ONE-PLANK
WOODWORKING
PROJECTS

ONE-PLANK
WOODWORKING
PROJECTS

ANDY STANDING

THE GUILD OF MASTER CRAFTSMAN PUBLICATIONS

First published 2012 by
Guild of Master Craftsman Publications Ltd
Castle Place, 166 High Street, Lewes,
East Sussex BN7 1XU

Publisher: Jonathan Bailey
Production Manager: Jim Bulley
Managing Editor: Gerrie Purcell
Senior Project Editor: Wendy McAngus
Editor: Simon Smith
Managing Art Editor: Gilda Pacitti
Designer: Robert Janes
Photography: Anthony Bailey and Andy Standing
Illustrator: Simon Rodway

Set in ITC Avant Garde Gothic
Colour origination by GMC Reprographics
Printed and bound in China by Hung Hing Printing Co Ltd

FOREWORD

Making and creating things is a wonderful way to satisfy the creative urge that is innate in most of us. Producing items for your home and garden is also a great way to express yourself and personalize your living space.

Woodworking is one such way of making things you can be proud of and you need only a basic toolkit and a few accessories to be able to do some wonderful work. Of course, most of us do some DIY, repairing and fitting things, but you can use your existing set of tools to help you make individualized projects for specific areas.

This book shows how to make 20 such projects in easy-to-follow steps that will help build your confidence as well as showing the basics of construction that underpin making any such projects.

Just be warned! Woodworking is fun and if, like me, you catch the woodworking bug then you will no doubt go on to make many more items for friends and family. Have fun!

Mark Baker
Editor, Woodturning & Woodcarving magazines

CONTENTS

Projects

INTRODUCTION

So what can you make with one plank? A floorboard, perhaps, or a shelf?
Well, with a bit of imagination, there is a lot more that you can do.

The aim of this book is to provide you with some plans and inspiration to construct a range of useful and functional items for the home and workshop, but without the need for complicated lists of materials. All are made using prepared timber, which can easily be obtained from your local supplier.

Each project can be made from a single plank with the occasional need for some hardware such as bolts or hinges, and perhaps the odd piece of sheet material such as plywood.

Construction techniques are straightforward, mixing both traditional timber jointing with more modern methods. The projects can all be made using hand tools alone, though using power tools will obviously speed things up a bit.

Many of the projects may also be modified to suit your particular needs. Don't feel that you must stick to the published dimensions. You might want a plate rack with more spaces, or a bigger rocking chair. If so, simply scale up the plan as you like. It is important, not only to make what you want, but also to enjoy the experience, and perhaps it will inspire you to start designing and making your own projects.

BASICS

CHAPTER ONE

TOOLS AND EQUIPMENT

Successful woodworking relies on many factors, and one of the most important is your toolkit. To complete any project, you will need a range of tools, and whenever you buy any, always choose the best that you can afford. Good-quality tools are expensive, but the money is never wasted, as they will give you years of service if properly cared for, and their superior quality will make them easier to use. Cheap tools are invariably a false economy, as they will be poorly designed and made from inferior materials, resulting in poor performance and disappointing results.

A well-equipped workshop will house a range of hand tools, power tools and possibly a few machines. However, for the novice woodworker it can all seem a bit daunting, so here is a guide to a range of tools that you can use to make the projects in this book.

HAND TOOLS

You will need a small selection of hand tools as well as measuring and marking instruments.

MEASURING AND MARKING

For general measuring, use a flexible steel tape or a steel rule. A try square and a combination square are useful for marking out, and a protractor and sliding bevel are needed for marking angles. A compass is also useful, as is an inexhaustible supply of pencils.

Tools for measuring and marking

SAWS

A selection of saws is useful. A hardpoint saw can be used for both ripping and crosscutting. For finer crosscutting, a tenon saw is used – although you may prefer to use a pullsaw, which, as the name suggests, cuts on the pull stroke. This means that it does not need stiff blades and can have thin, flexible ones with razor-sharp Japanese-style teeth that cut a thin kerf with great accuracy.

These saws are all designed to cut in a straight line, but for making curved cuts a coping saw is used. This has a metal frame across which a narrow blade is stretched. The orientation of the blade can be adjusted in the frame, so that the saw can cut in any direction. The blades are fragile and easily broken, but they are cheap to replace.

Selection of saws

PLANES

Once you have sawn your timber, you need to smooth the edges and correct any problems. A plane is the tool for this. Planes are made in a bewildering array of styles and sizes, from immense jointer planes through to tiny shoulder planes. However, to get started you only really need two: a smoothing plane and a block plane.

Smoothing and block planes

CHISELS

You will find a small set of chisels extremely useful. A well-sharpened chisel is a versatile tool capable of a range of functions from cutting joints to shaping details. Choose bevel-edged examples.

HAMMERS AND MALLETS

For workshop use, when making small projects, a heavy hammer is rarely needed – a medium-weight hammer for general use along with a pin hammer should meet all your needs. A mallet is also handy for driving chisels and persuading reluctant joints to cooperate.

Set of chisels

Selection of hammers

SCREWDRIVERS

There are many designs of screwdriver and a variety of blades to fit different screw heads. A sensible choice is one with a ratchet handle and interchangeable bits so that you can deal with a range of types and sizes of screw.

CLAMPS

These are extraordinarily important – without them you will find it difficult to complete your projects. A good selection is needed, with bar clamps for panels and larger assemblies and speed clamps, 'F' clamps and web clamps for all kinds of other jobs.

Selection of screwdrivers

Assorted clamps

POWER TOOLS

Power tools, whether mains-powered or cordless and battery-powered, greatly speed up your woodworking. A power drill really is a necessity, and a jigsaw is another tool that is worth investing in, not only for its curve-cutting ability but also for its versatility with the wide range of blades that are available. A circular saw will make short work of cutting up your boards, and you can also use a guide rail to improve accuracy.

POWER SANDER

A power sander eases the tedium of hand sanding and will give your projects a smooth, polished look. There are several different types of sander, but probably the most versatile is the random-orbit sander.

Random-orbit sander

SCREWDRIVER

For projects involving a lot of screwdriving, a powered screwdriver can be a real help. These are available in a variety of sizes to suit different jobs, but even the smallest are surprisingly powerful.

Cordless screwdrivers

Jigsaw and blades

Power drills

ROUTER

For any serious woodworker there is one tool that must be in the workshop, and that is the router. A router and router table allow you to undertake a wide variety of processes, from applying simple edge mouldings to cutting joints. For these projects a small router with a modest selection of cutters will be enough, and a simple router table will greatly simplify some operations.

Router

Biscuit jointer

BISCUIT JOINTER

The biscuit jointer is an extremely handy tool. It is simple, fast to use and can strengthen all manner of joints in moments. For all the projects in this book, No. 20 biscuits should be used unless otherwise stated.

WORKSHOP MACHINERY

If you become more serious about your woodworking, you will probably want to invest in some workshop machinery. This obviously demands a certain amount of workshop space and a fairly hefty financial outlay. However, it will raise your woodworking capabilities, allowing you to tackle large projects, and increase your speed and accuracy.

TABLE SAW

The first machine that most woodworkers acquire is a table saw, perhaps the most important machine in the workshop. It can be used both to rip and crosscut timber and make angled and bevelled cuts with ease and accuracy. The table saw is simply a circular saw mounted under a metal table. It is fitted with a pair of fences, one for ripping along the grain and a sliding fence for crosscutting. Larger saws have sliding tables to support the timber more effectively when crosscutting. The crosscut fence may be turned for cutting mitres and other angled cuts, and the blade itself can be tilted to perform bevel cutting.

Table saw

BANDSAW

Along with the table saw, the bandsaw is also a good investment – in fact, many home woodworkers prefer bandsaws to table saws. This is down to several factors: first, they don't take up much floor space; second, they run quietly, unlike table saws, so are less likely to annoy the neighbours; and finally, they are much less intimidating to use than a table saw, as there is no spinning blade and consequently little danger of kickback (when a workpiece is caught by the blade and then hurled back at the operator). Bandsaws are particularly good for producing curved components and are also great jointing machines. They are not as good as table saws at producing long straight cuts, but a well set up saw with a sharp blade will be able to do an acceptable job.

● ● ● **ONE-PLANK TIP:**

Cutting up the timber is just one of many jobs when making any project. You will also need to shape, joint, drill and assemble the piece.

Bandsaw

COMBINATION SANDING MACHINE

A combination sanding machine is an enormously versatile tool. With a sanding belt and a sanding disc, it can be used for smoothing and shaping both curved and straight-edged components.

PILLAR DRILL

A pillar drill greatly improves your drilling accuracy. Although a hand-held drill is fine for most jobs, when it comes to drilling perfectly accurate holes that are exactly perpendicular to the workpiece, you need some help. A pillar drill, or simply a power drill mounted in a stand, will do the job.

Combination standing machine

Power drill in a drill stand

CHAPTER TWO

TECHNIQUES

Woodworking is a disciplined process, and it is important to approach it methodically. If you work through projects logically, mistakes are less likely to occur – and as you familiarize yourself with the various processes, your skills will improve.

Start every project by selecting your materials and roughly marking out how to make the most economical use of them. Each plank should be marked so that you know which bit of the timber each component should be cut from. The next step is always to crosscut the components to length and then rip them to width. After that you continue with planing, shaping, jointing and assembling.

MEASURING AND MARKING

The first job on any project is to mark out your timber ready to be converted into the various components, and it is easy to make mistakes at this stage that will affect how successful your project will be. There are few things more irritating than misreading a measurement and consequently cutting your timber to the wrong size. There is a saying, 'Measure twice, cut once', and this is certainly very good advice.

You need to be disciplined and methodical in your marking. First, check your measurements and make sure that you are using the correct system. Don't mix metric and imperial – which can be easy to do by mistake, particularly if you have converted from one to the other.

Second, always use a clean, clear rule so that the markings are easy to see, and mark the timber with a sharp pencil or marking knife using a try square or a combination square. Carry the line around the timber to help you keep your saw cut straight, and make sure that when you cut the timber you cut on the waste side of the line. This means that the marked line should still be visible on the cut component.

When making several identical pieces, do not measure each one separately as this greatly increases the chances of making a mistake. Measure and cut the first piece and then use it as a template to cut the others. That way you can't go wrong, assuming that you managed to cut the first piece accurately. It is also a good idea to always start by cutting the longest components for a project, because if you make a mistake it might still be possible to reuse the piece as one of the shorter components.

Professional craftsmen use devices called setting-out rods or story sticks, which are pieces of board onto which all the dimensions of a project are marked full scale. That way, the maker only needs to lay the timber on the board and mark off the correct dimensions without any need for further measuring.

When marking curves and rounded edges, instead of struggling with a compass it is often easier to use a round object as a template – saucepan lids, paint pots, jars and even coins are all good for this.

1 Mark across the face using a try square.

2 Carry the line around the edge.

3 Copy marks from one workpiece to another.

4 A pair of identically marked components.

SAWING

Most people know how to saw through a piece of timber, but it takes practice to do it accurately and consistently. The first thing is to use the correct grip. Don't hold the saw too tightly, and make sure that your index finger is pointing forward along the side of the blade. This helps to keep your forearm in line with the blade and make the sawing motion much more even.

To begin a cut, first place the blade on the timber on the waste side of the marked line. Use the thumb on your other, non-sawing, hand to support the blade. Pull the blade gently towards you. Repeat this once or twice until it has started to cut into the timber. Now move your thumb away and start to move the saw backwards and forwards in the cut, progressively increasing the length of the stroke until you are using the entire length of the blade. Keep an eye on the marked lines to ensure that you keep the cut accurate. Saw slowly and smoothly and let the saw do the work.

1 The correct saw grip.

2 Guide the saw with your thumb as you pull back to start the cut.

3 Once the cut is established, move your hand away and continue to saw through.

4 The completed cut. Note that the marked line is still visible on the workpiece.

TIMBER CUTS

There are two different types of timber cuts. The first is rip cutting, which is when you cut parallel to the grain of the timber as you cut along a board. The second is crosscutting, which is when you cut across the grain of the timber as you cut a board to length. The two different cuts technically require two different saws, because when you are ripping along the grain you are actually splitting the wood fibres apart, which needs large, coarse, widely spaced saw teeth; crosscutting, however, severs the wood fibres and needs smaller, finer teeth to produce a good finish. These days, however, you can tackle both types of cut using modern hardpoint saws, which have considerably more sophisticated tooth geometry than more traditional tools.

When cutting timber, it is essential that it is properly supported. For ripping large boards, sawhorses are traditionally used; alternatively, a portable workbench can do the job. For crosscutting smaller components on the bench, a bench hook is used. This is a simple homemade jig with a cross batten to support the timber as you cut it. For end-grain cutting, the timber can be held in a bench vice.

A homemade bench hook

Ripping a board with the timber held in a portable workbench

SHARPENING YOUR TOOLS

Successful woodworking relies to a great extent on sharp, well-maintained tools. Blunt tools produce poor results and are far more likely to lead to accidents and mistakes, as their reluctance to cut easily makes the user exert excessive pressure on them, causing them to slip, spoiling the work and possibly injuring the user. Tool sharpening is a subject that can, and does, fill whole books. However, for the purposes of this book, it is only necessary to cover the basic sharpening of planes and chisels.

When you buy a new plane or chisel, it will not be ready for immediate use without some initial preparation. The blade will leave the factory having only been fairly coarsely ground, but to produce a high-quality finish, a razor-sharp edge is needed. This is not difficult to achieve, as all you need is a good flat sharpening stone.

The initial grinding angle on the blade is normally 25 degrees. Some woodworkers simply polish up this bevel and then use the tool, but this means that the blade has a rather weak edge, which can be easily damaged and will then be time consuming to sharpen. Better practice is to hone a secondary bevel on the blade at an angle of around 35 degrees. The advantage of this is that it produces a stronger edge and can be quickly resharpened, as only a tiny amount of metal will need to be removed.

1 A coarsely ground blade in need of honing.

2 To sharpen your blades, begin by flattening the back of the blade. Lubricate your stone, if necessary, then lie the blade on it, bevel up, and rub the blade along the stone while keeping an even pressure on it.

3 Continue until the back is smooth and evenly shiny.

4 Turn the blade over, bevelled side down, and rock the blade until you can feel that the bevel is flat on the surface. Now lift it slightly onto its tip in order to hone the secondary bevel. Keep the blade at this angle as you rub it up and down the stone.

5 Once you have managed to hone an even bevel about 1/32in (1mm) wide, stop. Now, if you feel the rear of the blade with your thumb, you will notice that you have raised a burr, which needs to be removed before the tool can be used. Do this by lying the blade down on the stone again, bevel up, and rub it a couple of times. Your blade is now ready for use. A really sharp blade should be able to shave the hairs from the back of your hand.

● ● ● ONE-PLANK TIP:

If you are finding it difficult to hold the blade accurately while you hone the secondary bevel, you can always use a honing guide. This is a small jig that attaches to the blade and holds it at the correct angle while you rub it along the sharpening stone.

PLANING

Once you have cut your timber, the next stage is to plane it. This smooths the timber and removes any imperfections such as the marks left by the saw blade.

SETTING UP YOUR PLANE

Planes are sophisticated tools and can appear a little intimidating to the novice user. But, when properly sharpened and set up, a plane can be one of the most pleasurable tools to use as you sweep off wafer-thin shavings from your timber and expose a perfect surface.

1 The first thing to do when you get a new plane is to dismantle it, sharpen it and set it up.

2 To reassemble a bench plane, first take the blade and hold it bevel down. Lay the cap iron across the blade so that the large screw drops through the hole in the blade.

3 Slide the cap iron up the slot and turn it so that it is correctly orientated on the blade.

4 Slide it down so that the front edge is about $\frac{1}{32}$in (1mm) from the blade edge.

5 Tighten the screw using the lever cap. This assembly then sits on the frog, which is the sloping part on the top of the plane.

6 The cap iron is on top of the blade and then the lever cap is placed on top of the cap iron to hold everything in place. With the plane inverted, turn the blade-adjustment knob until the blade just protrudes through the sole. Use the adjusting lever to set the blade parallel to the sole. There should be a small gap in the sole just in front of the blade to allow the shavings to be ejected. The size of this gap can be adjusted by removing the blade assembly, loosening the frog and moving it along the plane body.

USING A PLANE

Planing should not be hard work – the plane should slice cleanly through the timber without much resistance. You will need to adjust the blade to suit each piece of timber, but that just involves using the adjuster knob to set the blade protrusion.

1 Clamp your timber firmly in a vice or against a stop on the bench. Grasp the plane firmly by its handles and run it across the surface of the timber. Start with a little pressure on the front handle to initiate the cut and, as you move along the timber, transfer the pressure to the rear to avoid the plane tipping downwards as it comes off the timber. Try to plane the timber with the grain. This means that you with achieve a much better finish with less risk of any rough spots.

2 To determine the correct planing direction, look at the side of the timber. You should be able to see the angle at which the grain rises to the top. Plane in the same direction. Alternatively, if you run your finger along the top of the timber in both directions, you should be able to feel that one feels a little smoother than the other. That is the direction to plane in.

CHISELLING

In the home workshop, chisels can often be rather abused – they do, after all, look a bit like screwdrivers, and they are so good for opening cans of paint! However, this is not the way to treat your tools.

There are various kinds of chisel, but the most common is the bevel-edged design, which has bevels formed on both its sides making it versatile and useful in tight corners. Chisels are mainly used for chopping away waste material in joints but are also useful for shaping, trimming, cutting in hinges and a variety of other jobs. The most important thing about a chisel is that it should be razor sharp. A sharp chisel will cut easily and produce a good finish with minimal effort, but a blunt chisel may tear the wood and needs considerably more force behind it to cut into the timber.

Contrary to popular belief, chisels are not always used with a mallet. Most often you will use just the power of your hand to propel the tool through the timber to pare away the waste. You would use a mallet when removing the waste from a mortise joint or cutting in a hinge. Whenever you use a chisel, make sure that the workpiece is properly secured in a vice or clamped to the workbench, and make sure that if the chisel slips it cannot injure you.

Always clamp your workpiece securely to the workbench and carefully pare away the waste

POWER TOOLS

Although all the projects featured in this book can be made using hand tools alone, some power tools would make the job considerably easier. Here is a selection of the ones that can be most useful.

DRILL

The most familiar power tool is the drill, which can be bought very cheaply and is invaluable for drilling holes and running various useful accessories such as sanding drums. Now, of course, battery-powered cordless versions are available, which are really convenient. You will also need a set of drill bits. Twist drills can be bought in both metric and imperial sizes. It is important not to mix the two.

Power drills are relatively safe tools to use provided you follow basic safety procedures. Make sure that the workpiece you are drilling into is securely clamped to the bench or held in a vice. Hold the tool tightly and make sure that you are drilling straight. If you are not sure, stand a try square on the bench to use as a guide. With mains-powered drills, make sure that the cable is safely out of the way so that you cannot trip over it or drill through it.

One accessory that is particularly useful is a drill stand. This allows you to mount your drill vertically to ensure that your holes are perfectly accurate.

JIGSAW

The powered jigsaw takes the hard work out of cutting curved components. It can be used for both internal and external curves and can also cut a wide range of different materials when equipped with the right blade. Like any cutting tool, jigsaws must be used with care. Always make sure that the power cable is above the workpiece so that there is no chance of cutting through it. Also check underneath the workpiece before you start cutting. It is all too easy to clamp your work to the workbench and then wonder why your timber is so hard to cut, only to find that you have been cutting into the bench as well.

The majority of modern jigsaws have variable-speed motors that are controlled by the trigger. This makes them easy to work even in inexperienced hands. The secret to using a jigsaw accurately is to make sure that you steer it carefully, pivoting around the blade. Never put any sideways pressure on the blade, as it will result in a sloping, inaccurate cut that will spoil your work.

Cleaning up a curve with a drum sander mounted on a cordless drill

Cutting out a circular hole with a jigsaw

The finished hole

ROUTER

The router is an enormously capable machine that can perform a wide range of woodworking functions, including jointing, moulding, shaping and rebating. However, for the projects in this book its use is mainly limited to some simple moulding, using bearing-guided cutters.

The router can appear intimidating to the novice with its exposed cutters and high-pitched whine, but once you understand its workings and the techniques for using it safely, you will find it is not a difficult machine to master.

There are two main components in the router: the body and the base. The body houses the motor, the variable-speed electronics and the power switch. The base supports the body on a pair of sprung steel columns that allow the body to rise and fall as required to plunge the cutter into the workpiece.

Cutters

Before using a router, you need to understand a little about the cutters and how their rotation affects performance. The cutter rotates in a clockwise direction when viewed from above, which means that if you plunge a cutter into a workpiece and then push the router away from you, it will have a tendency to pull to the left. So you must fit the side fence to the right-hand side of the tool to counteract this. However, some operators prefer to pull the router towards them, and if that is your preferred method, you will need to fit the side fence to the left-hand side of the machine.

When edge moulding, where only one side of the cutter is in contact with the workpiece, you must always work against the direction of rotation so that the router is pushing back against you. This means if you were putting an edge moulding around the outside of a workpiece, you would have to move the router in a clockwise direction. However, if, for example, you were moulding the inside of a frame, you would have to run the router anticlockwise.

Setting up your router

If you have not had much experience of routing, it is worth practising some simple cutting on a piece of scrap timber or MDF to get a feel for the machine.

1 Clamp a short length of board to the workbench with its edge just overhanging the bench front. Draw a line parallel to the long edge about 4in (100mm) in from the front.

2 With the power disconnected, invert your router and fit it with a small straight cutter of around ¼in (6mm) in diameter. Make sure that at least three-quarters of the length of the cutter shank is inserted into the collet. Tighten securely.

3 Now loosely fit the side fence to the right-hand side.

4 Stand the disconnected router on the workpiece and plunge the cutter so that it is just touching the surface. Engage the plunge lock and move the router until the cutter is aligned with the marked line on the board. Adjust the fence so that it is tight against the front edge.

5 Now you must set the depth of cut. Leave the cutter touching the workpiece and wind down the depth-adjusting rod until it touches the top of the turret on the base plate. Now zero the scale, if possible, and wind the rod up by 5/32in (4mm). Lock it in this position and then release the plunge lock on the router so that the body rises up on the springs, lifting the cutter off the surface.

6 Check the speed control. For a small-diameter cutter, like the one shown here, the router can be run at full speed. For larger-diameter cutters the speed should be reduced. Check that all the adjustment screws are tight on the fence and on the depth-of-cut setting rod.

7 Position the router on the workpiece at the point that you wish to start the cut. Make sure that the fence is hard against the edge. Grasp the router by both handles and start the motor. When it has reached full speed, press down on the handles to plunge the cutter into the work and engage the plunge lock. Immediately start pushing the router forwards to cut the groove.

8 When you reach the end, release the plunge lock, allow the cutter to rise out of the work and switch off the motor.

Table routing

As well as hand-held, the router can also be used mounted beneath a router table. This method is particularly handy when moulding smaller components, and also when using large moulding or jointing cutters that cannot safely be used by hand. The same set-up rules apply to table routing as to hand-held routing, although in this case the router remains stationary in the table and the workpiece is pushed past the cutter, supported by the fence. It is important to use all the guards provided with the table, as they will protect you from the spinning cutter and also help support the work as it is machined.

• • • ONE-PLANK TIP:

At first it can be difficult to tell how fast to move the router when making a cut. You should not be forcing the machine along faster than it can cut, as this will strain the cutter and the motor. The motor should be running smoothly, and the router should move forward easily. If you move too slowly you will find that the cutter overheats and starts to leave burn marks on the workpiece. When making particularly intricate cuts, it can be easier to move the router slowly. In this case, use the variable-speed control to reduce the cutter speed.

A router table in action

BISCUIT JOINTER

The biscuit jointer is a very useful machine. It is fast and straightforward to use and very safe. It will cut strong joints in a moment, without the need for any complicated jigs or setting up. It is basically a small plunge saw that cuts slots into which dried, compressed beech ovals, called biscuits, are glued. The application of a water-based glue such as PVA causes the biscuit to swell in the slot creating a remarkably strong joint. Biscuits are ideal for edge jointing when making up wide boards from narrow sections. They can also be used instead of more complex joints, such as the mortise and tenon, in lighter constructions.

To use a biscuit jointer it is just a matter of adjusting the front fence so that the slot is cut in the centre of the thickness of your timber. So if your timber is ⅘in (20mm) thick, set the fence to ⅖in (10mm). Be careful to hold the tool level when you cut the joint, otherwise the two halves will not line up properly.

When setting out biscuit joints, it is not critical that they are exactly spaced, so you can just use a pencil and do it by eye – but be careful not to place biscuits too close to the ends of boards, as they can become exposed by subsequent trimming. Leave a gap of at least 2in (50mm).

1 Align the two boards to be joined and mark out the biscuit positions.

2 Carry on along the boards.

3 Clamp the boards to the edge of a bench and, holding the jointer horizontal, cut the joints.

4 The boards ready for assembling.

5 To make corner joints, stand the two components together and mark the biscuit positions.

6 Cut the joints in the end of the side piece.

7 Then cut joints in the face of the end piece.

8 The joint ready for assembly.

The completed joint

WORKSHOP MACHINERY

If you have the space then it's really worth investing in some workshop machinery. This will lift your woodwork to the next level and greatly improve your speed and accuracy.

TABLE SAW

The table saw is the mainstay of the professional workshop, and any serious woodworker with a large enough workshop should have one. A good table saw will convert your boards into finished components in a short time and with little effort. It will save a considerable amount of time and trouble. However, a table saw is capable of inflicting serious injury on the unwary, so it must be used correctly.

Setting up a table saw

The saw must be set up according to the manufacturer's instructions. It should be standing on a level surface with space all around to give you room to work.

The guards must be properly set and should never be removed. There are two primary guards on the table saw: the riving knife and the crown guard.

The riving knife is the curved metal piece that stands behind the saw blade. Its function is to hold the saw

cut, the kerf, open after the timber has passed the blade. The reason for this is that some timber can become case-hardened during the seasoning process, which means that when it is cut the internal stresses released can cause it to twist and move. If it should tighten around the back of the saw blade it can then be thrown back at the operator with considerable force. The riving knife protects you from this. It should be set about ⅛in (3mm) from the rear of the blade and should extend up to within ⅛in (3mm) of the top of the blade.

The crown guard is often mounted on the top of the riving knife and covers the upper part of the blade. It sometimes incorporates a dust-extraction outlet. Some crown guards are suspended over the blade without being attached to the riving knife.

Correctly set riving knife

Riving knife with a crown guard fitted

Suspended crown guard

Using a table saw

The table saw performs two basic functions: ripping and crosscutting. Whenever you use a table saw you must use a fence – it is not safe to run a workpiece past the blade freehand. Never let your hands get anywhere near the spinning blade – it is always better to use a push stick.

Before using the saw, check your workpiece for any nails, screws or lose knots. All these could damage the blade and will need to be removed. Next, set your fence. If ripping, the rip fence must be securely clamped and run exactly parallel to the blade. If crosscutting, the crosscut fence must be set at the correct angle. Start the motor and let the blade come up to speed, place the workpiece against

Using too fine a blade or feeding the timber too slowly will result in burn marks

the fence and feed it smoothly past the blade. You should be able to feel how fast to feed the workpiece: too fast, and the motor will struggle and the quality of cut will be poor; too slow, and the blade will leave burn marks on the timber.

When ripping long boards make sure that there is something to support the board as it comes off the back of the saw. Some saws have extension tables on the rear for additional support, while some people use a roller stand to support the timber. Alternatively, an assistant in the workshop could be the answer.

Check your fence accuracy with a try square

BANDSAW

The bandsaw is another popular workshop machine, particularly in home workshops. There are several reasons for this. The bandsaw is a safer, quieter machine than the table saw. As there is no spinning blade and the main thrust of the blade is downwards onto the table, there is no danger of kickback. The blade cuts a narrow kerf, meaning that there is less timber wastage, and it can also cut much deeper sections than a table saw.

Bandsaws can rip and crosscut and also cut curved components. It is also safe to use them freehand without any fences. However, for all its good manners, it must be remembered that a bandsaw is still a dangerous machine capable of causing serious injury, so you must always keep your hands well away from the blade.

Setting up a bandsaw

Bandsaws are not difficult to set up once you understand the basics. The blade is a continuous band that runs over a pair of wheels. The first job is to ensure that the wheels track correctly and that the blade runs smoothly and stays true. Next, you need to adjust the blade tension. Then, finally, the guides must be set correctly to give the blade adequate support. This is how you do it.

1 Isolate the machine from the mains supply and open the upper and lower doors. Loosen off the blade guides, both above and below the table, and slide them well away from the blade. Lower the upper blade guard so that it may be opened to release the blade. Release the tension on the upper wheel so that the blade is loose. Carefully lift the blade off the wheels and remove it. Wear gloves if you are worried about cutting your hands.

2 To fit a new blade, slide it into position and lift it onto the top and bottom wheels. Position it in the centre of the tyre and apply a small amount of tension until the wheels grip the blade.

3 Now turn the top wheel clockwise by hand and watch the blade run on the top wheel. If it stays in the centre, the tracking is correct; if it runs towards the front or the rear of the wheel then the tracking needs resetting.

4 To reset the tracking, adjust the knob that is mounted on the rear of the upper casing. This tilts the upper bandwheel until the blade runs true. Once this is done, apply some more blade tension until the blade feels secure. The tension is about right when the blade will deflect about ¼in (6mm) at the mid point with the guides fully raised. Some larger bandsaws have an integrated blade-tension indicator, which simplifies the process.

5 The blade correctly centred on the bandwheel.

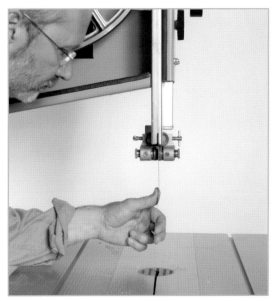

6 Checking the blade tension.

7 A blade-tension indicator is a great help.

8 Once you are sure that the blade is tracking correctly, move the guides into position. There are several different types of guide. Some manufacturers use plain metal guides, others use roller bearings. However, the same setting rules apply to both. The side guides should be set so that their front edges are just below the level of the blade gullets and they should be as close to the blade as possible without actually touching it.

9 The thrust bearing is the rear blade guide that supports the blade during cutting and stops it from being pushed off the bandwheels. Again, this should be set as close as possible to the back of the blade. It should only be in contact with the blade when the cut is taking place.

10 Once you are happy with the set-up, close the doors and start up the machine. Let it run for a moment to check all is well. While it is running you can fine-tune the blade tension until it is running at its smoothest. It is worth checking that the motor drivebelt is correctly tensioned. If your machine has several speeds, you should set it at its fastest for timber cutting. If your drivebelt is too loose, it can slip and cause vibration; if it is too tight, it will put unnecessary strain on the belt itself and the wheel bearings.

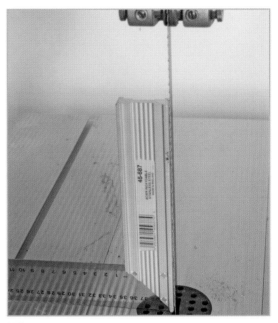

11 Use a try square to check the accuracy of the fences.

12 Also check that the table is set at 90 degrees to the blade and adjust accordingly.

Using a bandsaw

Bandsaws are satisfying machines to use. With the wide variety of blades available you can complete many tasks. Use wide blades when making long straight cuts and narrow blades for intricate curved work.

Set the upper saw guard so that the blade is covered as much as possible above the workpiece. This also brings the guide bearings down nearer to the cutting point, increasing the accuracy of the cut. Start the machine and push the timber through at an even speed – do not force it, just let the machine cut at its own pace. Be careful when cutting curves not to twist the blade too much as you may damage it or pull it off the bandwheels. Also, when making deep cuts that involve withdrawing the blade from the workpiece after the cut is made, make sure you stop the machine before withdrawing the blade – otherwise, again, you may pull it off the bandwheels.

Occasionally you might experience problems of blades wandering making it difficult to cut accurately. These problems are invariably caused by a worn or blunt blade, and replacing it with a new one should resolve it.

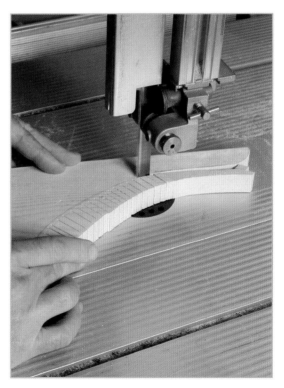

Curve cutting on the bandsaw

CHAPTER THREE

HEALTH AND SAFETY

The importance of workshop safety cannot be stressed too much. Careless use of sharp hand tools and electric power tools can lead to disaster. A poorly set up workshop can be a dangerous place, so take care to minimize the hazards with a little planning and some common sense.

WORKSHOP SAFETY

ELECTRICAL SAFETY

If you are using power tools or workshop machinery, you must make sure that both the tools and the electrical supply are safe. Your workshop wiring must conform to local regulations and have all the necessary protection systems installed. If you are in any doubt, you should employ a professional electrician to check it over.

Power tools can also wear out over time and become faulty. The main thing that can cause problems is the cable itself, as it takes a lot of punishment. It can get pulled, trodden on, cut and generally abused. Although cables are generally securely attached, they should be regularly checked and replaced when necessary. Never use a tool with a faulty cable. Keep your power tools and machines in good condition and always make sure that any safety guards are fitted and working. Replace any worn parts and keep blades and cutters sharp.

FIRST AID

It is worth keeping a small first-aid kit in the workshop with a few adhesive dressings and antiseptic cream, as even the most careful worker can sometimes cut a finger or get a splinter, and clean cuts do tend to bleed a bit – and you don't want blood stains on your work.

PERSONAL PROTECTION

In the workshop it is important to wear and use certain protective clothing to ensure your safety.

EAR PROTECTION

Woodworking can be a noisy process, particularly when using machines such as routers and planers. Protect your ears with a good set of ear defenders or earplugs. Some people might not like the feeling of isolation that these create, but to alleviate this problem you can use a set of ear defenders with an integrated FM radio, and these are a pleasure to wear.

A pair of standard ear defenders

Ear defenders with integrated FM radio

EYE PROTECTION

Even with all guards and protection in place, splinters and chippings can still be thrown up by power tools and other machinery. Powered jigsaws can be particularly problematic, as they cut from below the workpiece and then eject the sawdust upwards and straight into your eyes. A pair of safety glasses, or goggles if you prefer, will protect your eyes, and you can buy some that will fit over prescription glasses – so there is no excuse not to wear them.

Reflective safety glasses   *Safety eyewear to go over prescription glasses*   *Pair of goggles*

PROTECTING YOURSELF FROM SAWDUST

One of the biggest problems in the workshop is sawdust. Not only does it make a mess but it is extremely bad for your health if you inhale it, particularly if you use hardwoods.

Dust extraction

The solution to the problems caused by sawdust is to remove the dust at source by dust extraction. This need not be complicated. Most dust-producing power tools such as routers and sanders are supplied with adapters that can be connected to a workshop dust extractor. These are just industrial vacuum cleaners with special filters to capture the fine particles. They often also incorporate automatic switching systems, meaning that you connect your power tool to a socket mounted on the extractor and then when you switch on the tool the extractor starts automatically.

For larger stationary workshop machines, a bigger extractor may be needed with greater waste capacity. Many workshops have ducted extraction systems connected to all the machinery and controlled through a series of blast gates that direct the flow to the machine in use. However, this is an expensive and possibly unnecessary option for the home woodworker.

Workshop vacuum extractor

The power-tool socket and auto-switching controls on a workshop vacuum extractor

Large dust extractor suitable for a ducted system connected to workshop machinery

Dust masks

Even with good dust extraction, there are times when you will still need to wear a dust mask. This is particularly important when working with MDF, which produces a very fine dust, and also some exotic hardwoods, which produce dust that can be highly irritating. There is a wide range of masks, from simple disposable ones through to sophisticated respirator masks fitted with motors that blow filtered air across your face. It is a matter of finding one that is right for you – for example, if you have a beard you may find that some masks don't seal well on your face. As a rule, for short periods, disposable masks are usually more than adequate.

Powered respirator with face shield

Disposable dust mask

Dust mask with replaceable filters

THE PROJECTS

BOOKENDS

Bookends are always useful, and here is a simple design with an art deco feel that can be made with either hand or power tools. This is also a good project for using up any offcuts you may have lying around the workshop, as the quadrants can be made from contrasting timbers, which can look really attractive.

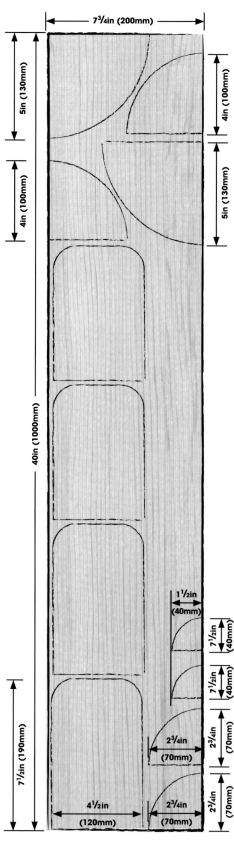

7³⁄₄in (200mm)

5in (130mm)

4in (100mm)

4in (100mm)

5in (130mm)

40in (1000mm)

1¹⁄₂in (40mm)

7¹⁄₂in (40mm)

7¹⁄₂in (40mm)

2³⁄₄in (70mm)

2³⁄₄in (70mm)

2³⁄₄in (70mm)

7¹⁄₂in (190mm)

4¹⁄₂in (120mm)

2³⁄₄in (70mm)

Begin by marking out your board as shown here

BOOKENDS

● ● ● YOU WILL NEED...

- Table saw or handsaw

- Jigsaw or coping saw

- Router table with straight cutter

- Clamp

- Wood glue

1 Prepare your plank as described on page 19. The quadrants can be accurately cut out using a powered jigsaw. Alternatively you could use a fretsaw or coping saw.

2 A table saw makes quick work of the other parts.

3 Take each pair of quadrants and clamp them together in a vice so that their square edges are aligned. Use a sanding block or a power sander to clean up the curved edge and smooth out any discrepancies.

4 The upright sits in a rebate cut into the base. Stand the upright on the end of the base with the edges aligned. Mark the width of the board with a pencil.

5 Make the depth of the rebate about two-thirds of the thickness of the board.

6 An easy way to cut the rebate is to use a straight cutter on a router table (as here). Alternatively you can cut the rebate using a tenon saw and chisel.

7 The corners of the bookends should be rounded. To do this, find something circular – a jar lid is ideal for the purpose – and position it on the corner. Mark the curve with a pencil.

8 There are various ways of rounding the corners. A disc sander is excellent. Alternatively, a bandsaw will do the job. If your bandsaw blade is too wide to make the curve, make some relief cuts around the curve first (as shown here), then the waste will fall away as you cut, freeing the rear of your blade. Clean up the curve with a sanding block.

9 Apply glue to the rebate and clamp the two components together. Make sure that they are set at right angles.

10 While the glue is curing, assemble the quadrants. These can be glued together in matching stacks. As long as the edges are square and the faces are smooth, apply a small amount of glue and simply stack up the pieces. There is no real need to clamp them.

● ● ● **ONE-PLANK TIP:**

When routing rebates, remember to take several shallow passes, not one deep one.

11 Finally, assemble the bookends, again with a little glue. The quadrants should be set back about ⅘in (20mm) from the front edge of the upright. Complete the project by softening all the edges with abrasive paper and then apply your finish of choice.

Your finished bookends should look like this when complete

DISPLAY SHELVES

Here is a simple project to make a pair of display shelves. It involves a lot of curve cutting and some moulding, for which you will need a router table. The moulding is purely for decoration, so leave it out if you prefer. However, do make sure that all the curves are smooth and that the corners are softened.

DISPLAY
SHELVES

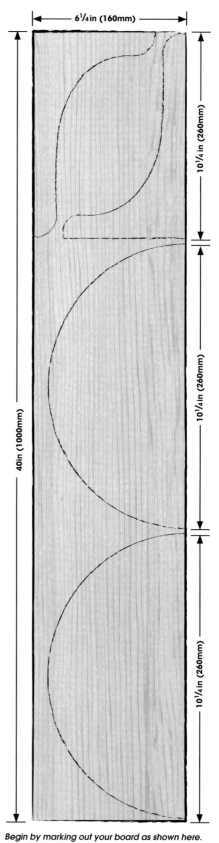

6¼in (160mm)

40in (1000mm)

10¼in (260mm)

10¼in (260mm)

10¼in (260mm)

Begin by marking out your board as shown here.
This plan shows components to make two display shelves

1 Prepare your plank as described on page 19. To draw the large semicircles for the shelves, use a scrap of ply with a hole for the pencil and a screw to pivot around. Draw out both shelves, but only draw the bracket for one. To do this, try to produce a pleasing freehand curve. This might take a few attempts.

2 Cut out the shelves using a jigsaw or bandsaw. Alternatively a coping saw could be used.

3 Cut out the bracket. If using a bandsaw, be sure to make some relief cuts so that the waste falls away as the cut progresses. Otherwise the blade can get twisted, particularly if it is on the wide side.

4 Smooth the inside curve of the bracket. A drum sander is ideal for this job.

5 Once you have sanded the bracket into a nice smooth curve, use it as a template to mark out the second bracket.

6 There are several ways to match up and create identical components. Here both shelves are clamped in the vice so they can be sanded or planed together to smooth out the curves and remove the saw marks.

7 Another option is to use one piece as the template for the other. Here the finished bracket and the sawn bracket are taped tightly together.

8 A bearing-guided trimming cutter is then used on the taped brackets, with the bearing running on the finished bracket and the cutter shaping the sawn bracket to match.

9 Mould the edge of the shelf, again using a bearing-guided cutter. An ogee cutter was used in this example.

10 The finished profile.

11 This is a corner bead cutter, which is a useful decorative tool. Use it to run a bead down each side of the bracket.

12 Do one pass on one side and one on the other.

13 Now the shelf can be assembled. Measure and mark the centre line across the underside of the shelf.

14 Drill two ⁵⁄₃₂in (4mm) holes through from the underside, on the line. Turn the shelf over and countersink the holes.

15 Put the bracket in the vice. Line it up carefully with the marked line, with its back flush with the back edge of the shelf. Fix with a pair of screws.

16 For neatness you can fill the screw holes with wood filler. Sand the filler flush when dry.

17 To hang the shelves, use a pair of mirror plates on each one. Chisel out a small recess in the shelf back so that the plate does not hold it proud of the wall. Screw into place.

Your finished display shelf should look like this when complete

TOY'S ROCKING CHAIR

Here is a design for a small rocking chair, ideal for the average teddy. However, there is no reason why you could not scale up the components to make a larger chair to suit a child. Drawing out the curved sides can be a bit of a challenge. An easy method is to take a sheet of paper and draw some experimental curves. When you find a shape you like, you can transfer it onto the timber by scribbling on the back face of the paper under the curve. Then lay the paper on the wood and draw along the curve again, so transferring the outline onto the timber.

TOY'S
ROCKING
CHAIR

● ● ● YOU WILL NEED...

- Table saw or handsaw

- Jigsaw or coping saw

- Drum sander

- Sheet sander

- Router table

- Biscuit jointer

- Wood glue

- Clamps

- Drill

- Screwdriver

- Pocket-hole jig

- Block plane

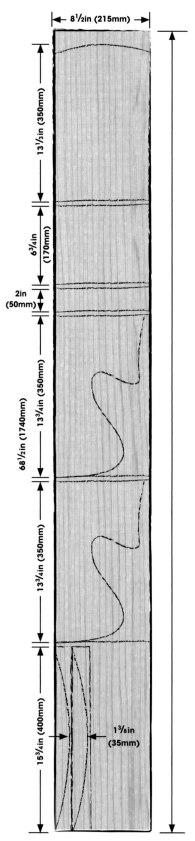

8¹⁄₂in (215mm)

13¹⁄₃in (350mm)

6³⁄₄in (170mm)

2in (50mm)

68¹⁄₂in (1740mm)

13³⁄₄in (350mm)

13³⁄₄in (350mm)

15³⁄₄in (400mm)

1³⁄₈in (35mm)

Begin by marking out your board as shown here

1 Prepare your plank as described on page 19. Once you've cut your wood, clamp both sides together and cut out the curve using a jigsaw (as shown here) or a coping saw.

2 The completed cut.

3 However good your cutting, the edges will still need smoothing. Use a drum sander on the internal curve.

4 And use a palm sander on the external curve.

5 The chair needs to sit at an angle on the rockers. Mark a point 1in (25mm) up from the rear corner of the side piece and then draw a line from the front corner up to this point.

6 You can cut both pieces at the same time by stacking them on the table saw (as here) and using an angled crosscut fence. Alternatively you can cut them separately using a handsaw.

7 The curve for the rockers has a radius of 24½in (620mm). To mark this, you can put a nail in your bench and use a long rule or a piece of string to draw the curve.

8 Cut the back panel roughly to length and mark a curve across its top. To do this make a mark on each side 1in (25mm) from the top,. Then, using a piece of string pivoting around the centre of the board, draw a curve through these two points and as close to the top edge as possible.

9 Cut out the rockers using a jigsaw or bandsaw (as here).

10 Clamp both rockers together and smooth them evenly on a belt sander.

11 Round the ends of the rockers on a disc sander.

12 Use the bandsaw again to cut the curve on the top of the rear panel.

13 All the components, including the seat and apron, are now cut out and ready for assembly.

14 Before assembling the chair, the edges of the main components need to be rounded over. Use a bearing-guided cutter mounted in a router table.

15 Carefully run the cutter around the front edges of the side panels, the top of the rear panel, the front edge of the seat and the bottom edge of the apron.

16 The back and sides are assembled using biscuit joints. Mark out the positions.

17 Cut the slots with a biscuit jointer.

18 Apply a little glue to the slots and insert the biscuits. Apply a little glue to the slots on the adjoining piece.

19 Assemble the back and sides and clamp up. Leave to dry.

20 The apron is attached to the underside of the seat, again using biscuits. Set it back about ¼in (6mm) from the front edge. Glue and clamp up.

21 The seat is held in position with pocket screws. Use a jig to drill two holes in each side.

22 Slide the seat into position and drive in the screws.

23 The rockers will be joined to the sides using biscuit joints. To disguise any discrepancies in the joint and to provide a straight shadow line, use a block plane to form a small chamfer on the bottom edge. You can also do the same on the outer edge of the rocker.

24 Mark the position of the biscuits on the sides and the rockers, and cut the slots.

25 Apply glue to the joints, assemble and clamp up.

26 You now have the completed chair. Carefully hand sand it to remove any rough edges and blemishes.

Your finished rocking chair should look like this when complete

KNIFE BLOCK

Kitchen knives can be difficult to keep handy, yet store safely. One of the most convenient ways to do so is to use a knife block like the ones that are supplied with expensive sets of knives. This is a surprisingly easy thing to make, which you can adapt to suit your own collection of knives.

KNIFE
BLOCK

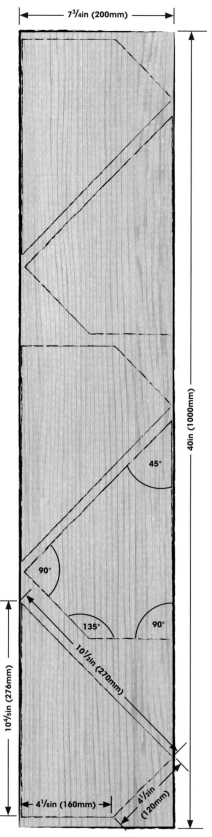

7³/₄in (200mm)

40in (1000mm)

45°

90°

135°

90°

10¹/₂in (270mm)

10⁴/₅in (276mm)

4¹/₈in (160mm)

4¹/₂in (120mm)

Begin by marking out your board as shown here

● ● ● YOU WILL NEED...

- Table saw or handsaw

- Smoothing plane

- Block plane

- Clamps

- Router with straight cutter and optional rounding-over cutter

- Wood glue

- Power sander

1 Prepare your plank as described on page 19. Cut out the parts using a table saw or handsaw. Inevitably there will be slight discrepancies between the parts, so clamp them all together in a vice and clean them up with a smoothing plane.

2 Use a block plane on the end grain.

3 Stand all the pieces together and mark a 'V' across the front so that you can reassemble the pieces in the right order after routing.

4 Mark out in pencil the positions of the knives you want to house in the block. Allow enough space so the blades will slide in and out easily. Start with the outer piece.

5 Then put the next piece on top and repeat the exercise.

6 Continue this process until the block is complete.

7 Extend the marked lines with a ruler and clearly indicate the areas to be cut out. These odd-shaped parts are difficult to rout using any kind of clamp, so position one on the front of the bench so that its edge just overlaps. Take a pair of timber or MDF offcuts and temporarily nail them onto the bench top to hold the piece in place.

8 Fit the router with the straight cutter. Set the cutting depth by plunging the cutter onto a flat surface, and then loosely sandwich one of the knife blades between the depth stop and the turret. Lock the depth stop.

9 Fit the router with its side fence and use the front edge of each the pieces to guide the tool as you rout out all the knife slots.

10 Apply glue to the pieces, being careful to avoid the knife slots.

11 Use the 'V' marking to ensure that you are reassembling the block in the right order and then clamp tightly. Leave to set overnight.

12 When dry, clean up the whole combined piece with a power sander.

ONE-PLANK TIP:

To keep the block clean it is a good idea to give it a couple of coats of varnish or oil. As a final touch, fit the base with a set of adhesive rubber feet to protect your work surface.

13 Finish by rounding over all the edges using the router fitted with a bearing-guided cutter. A routing mat on the bench should hold the block securely. Alternatively you could round the edges with a power sander.

Your finished knife block should look like this when complete

UMBRELLA STAND

In the past, no hallway would have been complete without an umbrella stand. Often an exotic and decorative object, it would be used to hold walking sticks and other paraphernalia as well as umbrellas. Here is a simple design to make a hexagonal stand. In order to cut the angles accurately for the joints, ideally you would need a good table saw. However, if you do not have one, you can cut the joints by hand and use a plane to smooth the edges to the correct angle.

UMBRELLA STAND

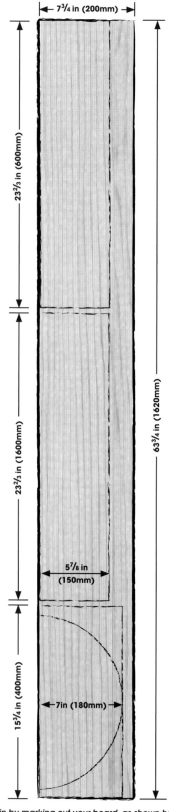

7³/₄ in (200mm)

23²/₃ in (600mm)

23²/₃ in (1600mm)

63³/₄ in (1620mm)

5⁷/₈ in (150mm)

15³/₄ in (400mm)

7in (180mm)

Begin by marking out your board, as shown here, twice. Note that your board must be long enough to take in two lots of these template shapes

1 Prepare your plank as described on page 19. Once you have marked up and crosscut your plank, you need to rip the edges of each side to an angle of 60 degrees. This must be accurately set, as any tiny discrepancy becomes magnified over six joints. The simplest way is to use a protractor and a sliding bevel to set your saw blade. However, if you have mislaid your protractor, there is another method. First, take a board offcut and rule a line parallel to one straight edge.

2 Then, take a pair of compasses and set the width about three-quarters of the length of the marked line. Mark an arc on the line and another above.

3 Using the same setting, insert the compass point where the arc and the line intersect and draw an arc on the other end of the line and another to intersect the upper arc.

4 Use a rule to join the three points and you will have an equilateral triangle, the internal angles of which are all 60 degrees.

5 Use the triangle to set the sliding bevel.

6 Use the bevel to tilt the saw blade to the correct angle.

7 Rip the first side of the board, with the fence set slightly wider than the finished width. You do this because you are going to cut the other side, and will need a little extra width to allow the saw to cut the bevel there.

8 Now set the fence to the exact width, turn the board round and rip the other edge. Repeat these two steps for all six sides.

9 Lay all the side panels edge to edge on the bench, with their outer faces downwards and their ends lined up. Mark two horizontal lines, one 3in (75mm) from the bottom and one 3in (75mm) from the top. These will be used to locate the biscuit joints.

10 With the panels still lying face down on the bench, cut a biscuit slot at each end on the pencil line.

11 Apply glue to the edges and into the biscuit slots, making sure that there is sufficient glue in the slots. Insert the biscuits and start the assembly.

12 Assemble two sets of three panels.

13 Fit the two sets of panels together.

14 Clamp together. Clamping up this kind of assembly is tricky, and the easiest method is to use web clamps or roof-rack straps. Wrap them tightly around the panels and make sure the joints are tight and the shape is true. Leave until the glue has cured.

15 After removing the straps, you will find that the corners are all very sharp. Use a block plane to smooth them down a little.

16 To form a chamfer around the edge of the stand, fit a bearing-guided chamfer cutter to the router (as shown). If you do not have a router, use a block plane instead.

17 Lie the stand on its side and carefully run the router around the top edge to cut the chamfer.

18 The base of the stand is made from a pair of boards jointed together. You can use biscuit joints if you like, but they are not really necessary. Just make sure that the two joining edges fit neatly without any gaps.

19 Use a pair of bar clamps to hold the boards while the glue cures.

20 Mark out the shape of the base on the board. The example here is a 14in (360mm) diameter, circular base – marked out with a pair of compasses – but a hexagonal base to match the stand will also work well.

21 A bandsaw was used to cut out this circle, but a powered jigsaw or coping saw could also be used.

22 To match the chamfer on the top of the stand, use the same cutter to run around the base. If you have an extended router base, it will make the router more stable and easier to control.

23 Stand the main body on the base and centre it by measuring in from the edge of the base to the corners of the stand.

24 Mark its position inside and out.

25 Remove the stand from the base and drill a clearance hole in the top of the base in the centre of where each panel will be positioned.

26 Countersink the holes on the bottom of the base. Invert the stand and place the base on top of it. Carefully line it up with the marks and then insert the six fixing screws.

Your finished umbrella stand should look like this when complete

KITCHEN SHELVES

You need a lot of storage space in a kitchen, and there are often little corners where you can fit a set of shelves. Here is a simple design that incorporates a rail for towels. It could be used for crockery or perhaps as a spice rack. The shelves have high front edges to stop things slipping off. A chrome hanging rail was used here, but a length of dowel will do equally well.

KITCHEN SHELVES

Begin by marking out your board as shown here

1 Prepare your plank as described on page 19. Mark out your plank. Both the sides and the shelves are the same length.

2 The shelves are narrower than the sides, so rip ⅜in (10mm) off the width. Also cut the two shelf fronts, but leave them overlong at this stage so you can trim them to fit accurately later.

3 Lay one shelf on top of one side panel and, with the rear edges lined up, mark the width of the shelf on the side. Repeat with the other side panel.

4 Mark the shelf positions on the side panels with a single line. They are set at 4in (100mm) from the ends of the sides. A good tip is to scribble on the side of the line where the housing is to be cut to avoid making a mistake and cutting on the wrong side. Lay both side panels on the bench, back to back, so that the shelf-width marks that you made are on the outside edges and the shelf positions are lined up. Lay a board across the bottom.

5 The board is to be used to guide the router when cutting the housing joints. Insert a ½in (12.5mm) diameter straight cutter in the router and set the depth of cut to ¼in (6mm). Clamp the board tightly across the end panels so the router runs exactly along the edge of the marked line. Cut the joint, being careful not to run over the end lines. Work from right to left. Then repeat the process for the second shelf.

6 The ends of the joints need to be squared off to match the shelves. Use a chisel for this.

7 The ends of the side panels are rounded. Use any convenient circular object as a template.

8 Cut off the corners using a coping saw (as here) or jigsaw.

9 Smooth the curves on a disc sander.

10 The towel rail sits in a pair of holes bored into – but not right through – the side panels. Mark the position of these 2in (50mm) in from the back and 2in (50mm) from the bottom.

11 Because the sides are thin, a flat bit cannot be used to bore the hole, so use the router instead. Fit a cutter to match your rail – a ⅘in (20mm) straight cutter was used here. Set depth of cut to ¼in (6mm). Fit the router side fence set to 2in (50mm) from the cutter centre. Position the router on the side panel and then use a clamp to hold it in place while you bore the hole.

12 The front edges of the side panels and the tops of the shelf fronts need to be rounded over. Fit a bearing-guided cutter in your router table.

13 Set the fence flush with the bearing.

14 Carefully round over the front, top and bottom edges of the side panels on both sides.

15 Round over the top edges of the shelf fronts.

16 It is worth cutting a rebate on the back of the shelf fronts. This makes fitting easier and provides a neater finish. Fit a straight cutter to the router table and set the height to the thickness of the timber.

17 Align the fence so that the cutter will take up to a ¼in (6mm) deep rebate.

18 This is a tricky cut to make because the workpiece is rather narrow, so use featherboards to hold it securely against the cutter.

19 Assemble the unit without glue to make sure that it all fits together. The towel rail should be the same length as the shelves. Hold it all together with clamps. Compare the diagonals to ensure that it is square.

20 The diagonals should both be equal. If they are not, loosen the clamps and adjust them to pull the frame into shape.

21 Offer up the shelf fronts and mark the correct length. Cut them to size.

22 Dismantle the frame and apply glue to the joints, then glue the shelf fronts on.

23 Reassemble, clamp up and leave to dry.

24 To fix to the wall, attach a pair of small brackets to the rear of the top shelf.

• • • ONE-PLANK TIP:

Always check projects for squareness when gluing and clamping up, as it is all too easy to over-tighten the clamps and push the assembly out of shape.

BATH RACK

There are few things nicer than a long soak in a hot bath after a hard day's work.

To help you make the most of your bathtime experience, here is a simple design for a bath rack that can hold all the necessities and perhaps prop up a book as well.

It is a fairly simple project to make, although there are some repetitive tasks where simple jigs or guides can help.

All $^{12}/_{32}$in (9mm) →

$2^1/_2$in (65mm)

$2^1/_4$in (60mm)

$18^1/_2$in (471mm)

$27^1/_2$in (700mm)

135°

$^4/_5$in (20mm)

$7^1/_2$in (190mm)

Begin by marking out your board as shown here

BATH RACK

1 Before you begin, check the measurements against the width of your bath and make any necessary adjustments. Prepare your plank as described on page 19. Start by cutting out the two side pieces. A bandsaw is ideal for this (as here), although a jigsaw or a handsaw would be fine.

2 Use a mitre fence to cut the 45-degree angles.

3 Mount a bearing-guided rounding-over cutter in your router table.

4 Machine the top edges of both sides.

5 The next job is to make the slats. These should be ⅓in (9mm thick) and 6¼in (160mm) long. Rip several lengths off the board. To be safe, you should always use push sticks when ripping narrow sections.

6 Crosscut the slats to length. You will need 20.

7 The slats will be fixed to the sides using screws. This means that they must all be drilled and countersunk at both ends. If you have a pillar drill, clamp a couple of offcuts to the table to act as guides to hold the slats in position. For best results, use a $\frac{5}{32}$in (4mm) drill bit with combined countersink.

8 Now all the slats must be carefully sanded. Unfortunately the only way to do this is by hand. Take care to remove all sharp edges and corners.

● ● ● ONE-PLANK TIP:

When making several identical components do not measure each one separately, but instead cut one accurately and use it as a template to mark out the rest.

● ● ● ONE-PLANK TIP:

To stop bath water spoiling the timber you can seal it with clear varnish or finishing oil.

9 The slats are fixed using ⁵⁄₃₂ x ⁴⁄₅in (4 x 20mm) screws. Start attaching the ones on each end, which will then hold the sides in position. Then simply arrange the remaining slats evenly along the rack. You can do this purely by eye, although if you want the spacing to be perfect you will have to work out the gap and make a spacer piece.

Your finished bath rack should look like this when complete

LAMP BASE

Table lamps can be remarkably expensive, so why not make your own?

Of course, many people choose to turn their lamp bases, but if turning is not your forte you need an alternative plan. Here is a simple design that is pretty easy to make. You will need to buy the electrical components and some paint, and a length of $5/16$in (8mm) threaded rod will also be helpful. Apart from that, you just need your plank. Choose a nice piece of hardwood, if you can. The plan here shows components to make a pair of lamps.

LAMP BASE

● ● ● YOU WILL NEED...

• Table saw or handsaw

• Bandsaw

• Pillar drill or hand drill

• Screwdriver

• ⁵⁄₁₆in (8mm) threaded rod

• Black paint

• Lamp holder

• Wood glue

7³⁄₄in (200mm)

40in (1000mm)

1¹⁄₄in (30mm)
⁵⁄₈in (15mm)
1¹⁄₄in (30mm)
⁵⁄₈in (15mm)
1¹⁄₄in (30mm)
⁵⁄₈in (15mm)
1¹⁄₄in (30mm)
⁵⁄₈in (15mm)
1¹⁄₄in (30mm)
⁵⁄₈in (15mm)
1¹⁄₄in (30mm)
⁵⁄₈in (15mm)
2¹⁄₃in (60mm)
⁵⁄₈in (15mm)
2³⁄₄in (70mm)
⁵⁄₈in (15mm)
3¹⁄₈in (80mm)
⁵⁄₈in (15mm)
3¹⁄₂in (90mm)
1in (25mm)
4in (100mm)
1in (25mm)
4¹⁄₃in (110mm)
1in (25mm)
4¹⁄₂in (120mm)

Begin by marking out your board as shown here.
This plan shows components to make two lamp bases

1 Prepare your plank as described on page 19. Any type of saw can be used to cut out the parts. Here a table saw is being employed.

2 A bandsaw is particularly good for cutting out the smallest blocks.

3 Clean up all the edges with sandpaper. Round the corners and soften all the edges so the parts are smooth to touch.

4 Each block needs a ⁵⁄₁₆in (8mm) hole drilled through its centre, here using a hand drill. It is important that this is accurately positioned and bored at precisely 90 degrees.

5 For greater accuracy, use a pillar drill or a power drill in a stand, if you have one.

6 To facilitate this you can make a simple jig, as here, to hold all the small blocks in position for drilling.

7 All the small blocks need to be painted black, so slide them onto the threaded rod.

8 Support the rod on blocks or small boxes and paint the edges.

9 Leave to dry.

10 To accommodate the electric cable, a groove needs to be cut in the underside of the base. A small carving gouge was used here, but a router fitted with a core box cutter would also do a good job.

11 The finished groove. Check that it is deep enough to contain the flex.

12 To assemble the lamp, clamp the threaded rod in the vice with a nut and large washer at the bottom.

13 Slide the base onto the rod so that it seats on the washer. Put a small amount of glue around the centre and then slide a black block down onto it.

14 Continue this process until the pieces are all on.

15 Experiment with different alignments if you like.

16 Once you are happy with the set-up, put another large washer on the top and screw a nut down tight on the assembly to hold it together while the glue cures.

17 Once the glue has cured, the rod can be removed. It can be a little reluctant to come out and a few taps with a hammer may be needed. Be careful to support the assembly properly so it is not damaged. Insert the flex and fit the lamp holder.

Your finished table lamp should look like this when complete

LAPTOP TRAY

Laptops are amazing machines, allowing you to work or play wherever you are. However, actually using them on your lap for any length of time can become uncomfortable – the base can get hot, and it can be cramped staring down at the screen – and some health issues have been associated with doing so. Here is a design for an adjustable laptop tray that will allow you to use your laptop anywhere in comfort.

LAPTOP TRAY

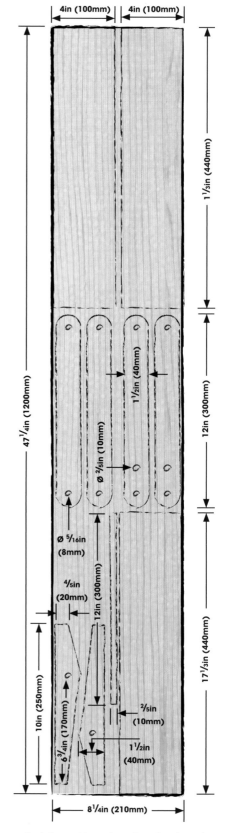

Begin by marking out your board as shown here

• • • YOU WILL NEED...

- Table saw or handsaw

- Plane

- Biscuit jointer

- Biscuits

- Hand sander

- Disc sander

- Drill

- Hammer

- Wood glue

- 4 x ⁵⁄₁₆in (8mm) pronged tee nuts

- 4 x ⁵⁄₁₆in (8mm) wing nuts

- 4 x ⁵⁄₁₆in x 2in (8 x 50mm) bolts plus washers

1 Prepare your plank as described on page 19. Once you have marked up and crosscut your plank, rip the components to size. For stability it is wise to make the tray from three strips jointed together as, if correctly orientated, this helps to reduce the timber's tendency to cup and distort. Plane the edges smooth.

2 Lay the tray boards side by side on the bench, making sure that they are arranged with the growth rings on the end grain running in opposing directions on each board. This helps keep the tray surface flat. Mark the positions for the biscuit joints.

3 Cut the joints with a biscuit jointer.

4 Glue the boards together. For maximum strength, make sure that the biscuits are generously supplied with glue.

5 Clamp up securely and leave to cure.

6 Once the glue has set, remove the clamps and clean up the surface with a sander. If it is uneven, use a smoothing plane first.

7 The tray corners need to be rounded off. Use any suitable circular object as a template to mark the corners. An aerosol lid was used here.

8 Remove the majority of the waste with a saw.

9 Then smooth the curve with a disc sander.

10 The four legs also have rounded ends. A large washer was used as a template here.

11 Mark the positions of the bolts and tee nuts, as on the plan. The double holes should be 2in (50mm) apart.

12 Bore ⁵⁄₁₆in (8mm) holes for the bolts and ⅖in (10mm) holes for the tee nuts.

13 The pronged tee nuts are inserted into the lower holes on the two legs and into the holes on the tray support bars.

14 You can either tap them into place with a hammer or press them in, either with a clamp or, alternatively, by inserting a bolt and using a large washer and a nut to pull the tee nut into the timber (as here).

15 Drill a pair of 5/32in (4mm) diameter holes in the tray support bars 1in (25mm) in from the ends.

16 Attach the support bars to the underside of the tray. Position them 1–1¼in (25–32mm) in from the sides.

17 To prevent your laptop sliding off the tray attach a small stop bar along the edge. This is ⅖in (10mm) square and 12in (300mm) long. Round off the top corners on the disc sander and use pins to hold it in position. Punch the pins below the surface and cover the heads with a dab of filler.

18 Assemble the tray as shown. If you find it difficult to tighten the wing nuts sufficiently to hold the legs tightly in position, make up some double-sided washers from abrasive paper and sandwich them within the joints to provide additional friction.

Your finished laptop tray should look like this when complete

PLATE RACK

There are many ways to store your crockery in your kitchen. You can pile it all up in cupboards, you can display it on a dresser – or you can use a plate rack. Here is a design for a plate rack that can be used as a freestanding unit, or, if you remove the top and cut off the feet, it could be fixed underneath an existing wall unit.

2/5in (10mm)

9⁴/5in (245mm)

⁴/5in (20mm)

12¹/2in (320mm)

19³/4in (500mm)

12¹/2in (320mm)

19¹/2in (500mm)

22⁴/5in (580mm)

80⁵/8in (2050mm)

4¹/16in (105mm)

1¹/2 in (40mm)

15¹/2 in (395mm)

1in (25mm)

15¹/2in (395mm)

8¹/2in (215mm)

Begin by marking out your board as shown here

PLATE
RACK

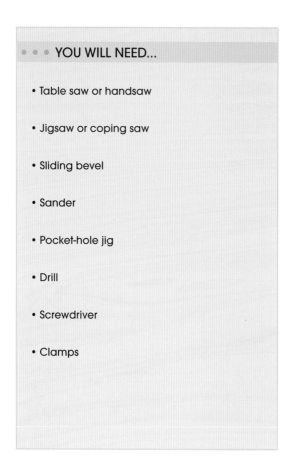

● ● ● YOU WILL NEED...

• Table saw or handsaw

• Jigsaw or coping saw

• Sliding bevel

• Sander

• Pocket-hole jig

• Drill

• Screwdriver

• Clamps

1 Prepare your plank as described on page 19. The rack obviously needs to fit your plates. This design is intended to fit 10½in (270mm) diameter plates. So take a plate and ensure that it will fit between the rails. Use two small offcuts from the rails to work out the spacing.

2 Mark out the positions of the rails according to the size of your plates.

3 The front edges of the rack have curved cutouts. A plate makes a good template.

4 Mark out the positions of the feet. Use a sliding bevel to mark the angle. The precise angle is not important, just choose one that looks right to you.

5 Clamp both sides together on the edge of the bench and cut out the front curve. A powered jigsaw is ideal for this (as here), or you could use a coping saw. Reclamp the boards and cut out the feet.

6 The rough edges of the saw cuts will need smoothing. Again keeping the sides clamped together, sand the edges smooth. A drum sander is ideal, but the detail sander shown here does a pretty good job.

7 Cut the four rails to length. To fix them to the sides pocket screws are used. Clamp each rail into the jig and bore holes in both ends. Make sure that you bore them on the same face.

8 Screw the rails in position. A batten has been clamped onto the workbench and the end panel is held against it. This makes it much easier to align the rails with the edges when you are screwing them down.

9 Crosscut another length of board and then rip the uprights to size.

10 Lay out the uprights in the rack and work out the spacing, referring to your plate again. Ten were used here with a spacing of approximately 1⅜in (35mm) between them. Both sides are identical.

11 The ends of the uprights need to be notched to locate them on the rails properly. Mark the position of the notches with a pencil.

12 Now mark a line across the centre of each upright to indicate the depth of the notch, and carefully cut out all the notches with a pullsaw.

13 The uprights are simply pinned onto the rear of the cross rails. Lay the rails out on the rack and, rather than measuring the space between them, make a spacer piece which will greatly speed up the fixing process.

14 The top is made from a pair of boards separated by a ⅝in (15mm) gap. These are fixed with three screws through the top rails. So drill and countersink the holes, then screw through into the boards.

15 The top boards also need fixing on their inner edges to stop them bowing up. A pocket screw in each corner is used. Wedge the drilling jig in place with a timber offcut pressed against it.

16 Insert the screws. If you do not have a small pocket-hole jig, the top can be fixed down using small metal brackets instead.

BREAKFAST TRAY

How lovely it would be to have breakfast brought to you in bed every morning. Unfortunately, for most of us it is a rare luxury. However, on those special occasions when it does happen, it is important to have the right sort of breakfast tray. A normal tray is hard to balance in bed and the last thing you want is a coffee-soaked sheet or marmalade on your pillow. Here is a design for a tray with folding legs that will stand securely on the bed with legs extended or can be used with the legs folded.

BREAKFAST
TRAY

9¼ in (235mm)

10¹/₁₆ in (255mm)

1¼ in (30mm)

²/₅ in (10mm)

10¹/₁₆ in (255mm)

2¹/₈ in (55mm)

²/₅ in (10mm)

13³/₈ in (340mm)

2¹/₈ in (55mm)

4in (100mm)

2¹/₈ in (55mm)

15in (380mm)

1in (25mm)

23²/₃ in (600mm)

68½ in (1740mm)

22in (560mm)

22in (560mm)

Begin by marking out your board as shown here

1 Prepare your plank as described on page 19. Mark out your plank, then crosscut to length.

2 Now rip the components to size.

3 The tray frame has mitred joints on the corners. These can be cut using a table saw or mitre saw. Alternatively you could use a tenon saw or a pullsaw (as here) and a mitre box.

4 The two ends have hand holds cut into their undersides. These should be about 4in (100mm) in length and 1in (25mm) high, so that your hands will fit comfortably. Mark them out with a pencil and try square.

5 Find a suitable template to mark the rounded corners. This can was ideal.

6 A jigsaw or coping saw can be used to cut the hand holds out.

7 Clean up the curves with a small drum sander.

8 The edges of all the components need to be rounded over. The simplest way to do this is to use a bearing-guided rounding-over cutter mounted in a router table. Remember not to round over the outer edges of the two outer boards of the tray, as they will be glued to the inside of the frame.

9 The boards will be biscuit jointed into the frame. Roughly assemble the tray and line up the boards. Mark the position of the joints on the boards and the frame. You will need one biscuit on the end of each board and three biscuits along the outside edges of the outside boards.

10 Set the jointer to cut your slots exactly in the centre of the boards' thickness. Cut the end joints on all boards and side joints on the outside boards.

11 Now reset the jointer fence so that it is ¼in (6mm) higher.

12 Cut the joints in the frame running the fence against the top surface.

13 Glue up the joints and assemble the tray. Be careful not to use too much glue in the biscuit slots as it will all squeeze out. Use enough to coat the biscuits thoroughly without too much overflow.

14 Clamp the assembly up tight. A web clamp will do, but make sure that the corners are square by measuring the diagonals and ensuring that they are the same.

15 Once the tray is complete and the glue dry, you need to fix the legs. Cut them to length and mark the ends for rounding over. A washer was used here.

16 Once all the ends have been rounded over, mark the position of the pivot screw. This should be about ½in (12.5mm) from the end.

17 Drill a ⁵⁄₃₂in (4mm) diameter hole in each leg. A pillar drill is a good choice for this as it is important for the hole to be perpendicular.

18 Attach the legs to the inside of the frame about ⁴⁄₅in (20mm) in from the corner. Use a screw and cup washer but do not overtighten it.

19 The legs need a crosspiece between them to provide additional stability. Drill pilot holes and countersink.

20 Fit the rails to the legs.

21 The completed tray folded.

Your finished breakfast tray should look like this when complete

FOLDING STOOL

Sometimes it is convenient to sit at your workbench, particularly when involved in intricate work. However, a stool takes up valuable floor space and can get in the way when you are not using it. Here is a simple design for a folding stool that can be stored in a corner – or even hung on the wall – when not needed.

FOLDING STOOL

• • • YOU WILL NEED...

- Handsaw or table saw

- Jigsaw, bandsaw or coping saw

- Router table

- Disc sander

- Drill

- Screwdriver

- Pair of back-flap hinges

12in (300mm)
2in (50mm)
2in (50mm)
4in (100mm)

26in (660mm)

40in (1000mm)

$2\frac{1}{3}$ in (60mm)

$7\frac{3}{4}$ in (200mm)

R: 5in (125mm)

Begin by marking out your board as shown here

1 Prepare your plank as described on page 19. Mark out your plank. Choose a sturdy board at least 1⅛in (28mm) thick.

2 Crosscut the end of the board and remove the seat.

3 You can cut out the seat disc in a variety of ways. A powered jigsaw is ideal, but a fret saw or coping saw can also be used. A bandsaw is being used here with a simple home-made jig that pivots the workpiece around a nail to produce a perfect circle.

4 Turn the workpiece slowly – and be sure to use a narrow blade.

5 The cut out seat.

6 Cut out the other components.

7 The edges of the seat need to be rounded over for comfort. A bearing-guided cutter mounted in a router table is ideal for this.

8 Mould both sides of the seat.

9 It looks good if you curve the tops of the two narrow legs, although this is not entirely necessary. If you do, mark out a curve with a suitable template.

10 Then sand off the edges with a disc sander.

11 Position the three legs on the stool with the two narrow legs vertical and the large central leg horizontal. The vertical legs should be as near to the edge as possible without hanging over it.

12 Use a pair of back-flap hinges to attach the legs, keeping the central leg in position to protect the spacing. Run a countersink into each hole before inserting the screw. This ensures that the screw is centrally positioned in the hole.

13 Clamp all three legs together so that they are exactly lined up. Mark a point 6¾in (170mm) down from the top and drill a ⅕in (5mm) diameter hole through each of the outer legs and into the central leg.

14 Use a ⅕ x 3⅛in (5 x 80mm) screw with screw cup to secure each outer leg to the central leg. Do not overtighten it, as it must be free to swivel.

15 Invert the stool and fix a stop block to the underside to support the central leg. Ideally angle the edge of it to match the slope of the leg.

16 The final job is to fit a bracing bar between the two outside legs. Take a 2⅓in (60mm) wide length of plank and reduce its thickness on the bandsaw to around ¾in (18mm). Trim to length (width of the three legs when laid flat).

17 Attach the bar to the legs with four 4 x 1¼in (30mm) screws with screw cups.

Your finished stool should look like this when folded

The stool should look like this when complete

WEATHERVANE

A weathervane adds the finishing touch to any building, from a garden workshop to a stately home. There are endless designs for weathervanes from the mundane to the surreal. Here is a very straightforward one with an arrow-shaped vane. Feel free to modify the design to suit your taste; however, there are two stipulations. First, one end must have a larger surface area to catch the wind and second, both ends must balance at the pivot point, otherwise the vane will not spin easily.

WEATHERVANE

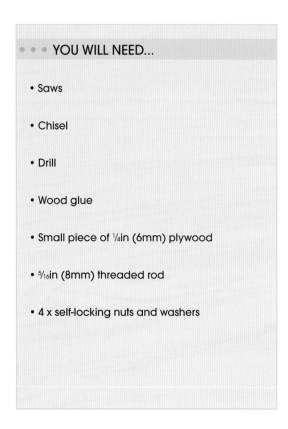

• • • YOU WILL NEED...

- Saws

- Chisel

- Drill

- Wood glue

- Small piece of ¼in (6mm) plywood

- ⁵⁄₁₆in (8mm) threaded rod

- 4 x self-locking nuts and washers

7¹⁄₈ in (190mm)

4¹⁄₂ in (120mm)

10in (250mm)

28¹⁄₃ in (720mm)

1¼in (30mm)

1¼in (30mm)

40in (1000mm)

1¹⁄₂ in (40mm)

9¹⁄₂in (240mm)

1¹⁄₂ in (40mm)

1¹⁄₂ in (40mm)

9¹⁄₂ in (240mm)

Begin by marking out your board as shown here

1 Prepare your plank as described on page 19. A table saw is good for ripping the straight components off the board.

2 A powered jigsaw will deal with the rest.

3 Cut the V in the rear of the vane.

4 The two side pieces are glued to the front end of the vane to balance it. Clamp them in place and allow time for the glue to dry.

5 The two crossbars are joined with a simple halving joint. Mark this out by finding the centre of each bar, then lay one across the other at right angles. Mark the width of the upper bar on the lower bar and the width of the lower bar on the upper bar. Now measure down to half the thickness of the bar and mark a horizontal line.

6 Make a series of parallel cuts down to the marked line with a tenon or similar saw.

7 Remove the cut pieces with a chisel.

8 The completed joint, which can be glued in place.

9 Drill a ⁵⁄₁₆in (8mm) hole through the centre of the joint for the threaded rod.

10 The next job is to make the indicators for the points of the compass. The simplest way is to print out the four letters from your computer. Try to find a simple font that will make the letters easy to cut out. They should be around 2in (50mm) high. Stick the prints onto ¼in (6mm) plywood with spray-on craft mount.

11 A bandsaw is a good choice for cutting out the letters, although a jigsaw or fretsaw can also be used.

12 The completed letters. Note the additional ⅖in (10mm) section on the base of each that will be used to mount them onto the crossbars.

13 Rout a ¼in (6mm) wide groove at the end of each crossbar to take the letters. The simplest way to do this is with a router table, as it is difficult to balance a hand-held router on such a narrow workpiece. Set the cutter depth to ⅖in (10mm).

14 Feed the ⁵⁄₁₆in (8mm) threaded rod through the crossbars and fix in place with a pair of self-locking nuts and washers. Allow at least 12in (300mm) to extend below the crossbars so that you can use it for mounting the completed wind vane.

15 To finish, the vane is mounted on the top of the rod between a pair of self-locking nuts and washers. Before you bore the hole in the vane, find the balance point by laying a pencil on the bench and placing the vane upright on it so that it will balance. Bore the hole at this point. The letters are glued into the grooves on the crossbars close to the end. A coat of black paint will make them stand out.

Your finished weathervane should look like this when complete

TOOLBOX

Carrying tools around can be a real bore. You can buy all kinds of toolboxes and bags, but why not make your own? You can make it to suit your tools and customize it to fit any special accessories that you might have. This toolbox is based on a traditional design but with a sliding tray that can be used for screws and small fixings.

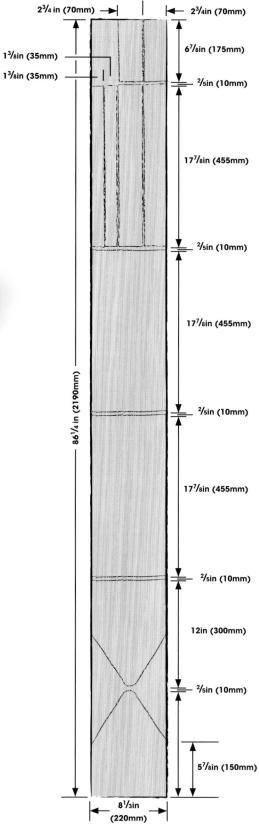

2³⁄₄ in (70mm)

2³⁄₄in (70mm)

6⁷⁄₈in (175mm)

1³⁄₈in (35mm)

1³⁄₈in (35mm)

²⁄₅in (10mm)

17⁷⁄₈in (455mm)

²⁄₅in (10mm)

17⁷⁄₈in (455mm)

²⁄₅in (10mm)

86¹⁄₄ in (2190mm)

17⁷⁄₈in (455mm)

²⁄₅in (10mm)

12in (300mm)

²⁄₅in (10mm)

5⁷⁄₈in (150mm)

8¹⁄₃in
(220mm)

Begin by marking out your board as shown here

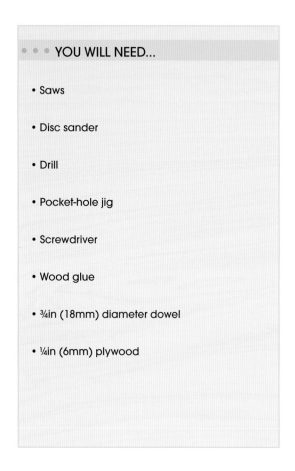

TOOLBOX

● ● ● YOU WILL NEED...

- Saws

- Disc sander

- Drill

- Pocket-hole jig

- Screwdriver

- Wood glue

- ¾in (18mm) diameter dowel

- ¼in (6mm) plywood

1 Prepare your plank as described on page 19. When making identical pieces, it is much easier and neater if you can deal with them as one, so tape the cut out ends together with masking tape and draw out the shape on the top piece. Cut off the waste.

2 To shape the curved top, a disc sander is ideal. Note that the pieces are still taped together.

3 A hole needs to be bored for the dowel handle. Use a flat bit and, again, keep the pieces taped together. Remember to put a piece of scrap board underneath to protect the drill bit and leave a clean exit hole.

4 Cut the baseboard and the shelf to length. The jointing on this box is very simple. Pocket screws were used here, but biscuits or simply screwing through from the end into the base would be equally effective. Use a jig to drill the pocket hole.

5 Assemble the sides and the base.

6 To make the tray, rip four pieces to suit. Cut them to length and check the fit. The tray should be snug in the base, but no too tight – this is not a cabinet drawer, after all.

7 For the base of the tray a piece of ply is used. This will sit in a groove cut with a straight cutter into the inside faces of all four sides of the tray. Use a ¼in (6mm) straight cutter at a depth of ¼in (6mm), with the fence also set to ¼in (6mm) back.

8 Pocket screws were used to hold the tray together here – a double pocket jig was used for speed. Alternatively you can just screw through the corners into the end grain.

9 Loosely assemble the tray and measure the inside length and the inside width. Add ½in (12mm) to both these dimensions and cut a piece of ply to this size.

10 Assemble the tray.

11 The simplest way to fit the shelf and make sure the tray can slide in and out smoothly is to put a couple of spacers on top of the tray edges. A couple of pieces of thick abrasive were used here. Lay the shelf in position.

12 Screw through the ends to hold the shelf in position. Fit a pair of side pieces on the shelf in the same way.

13 A piece of dowel is used for the handle. To ensure that it is a tight fit in the hole, cut a slot in each end, and make a pair of wedges.

14 Fit the dowel and hammer the wedges into position. Trim the ends and smooth off with a sander.

15 Use a scrap of timber to make a pair of rotating catches to stop the tray from falling out. Screw in position on each side with a screw cup. Do not overtighten, as the catches must be free to swivel.

16 You can make special holders for your tools, like this grooved piece to hold a saw, which is simply glued in place.

17 You can also make holders for your drill bits by taking a small timber offcut and using each drill to bore its own storage hole. Then simply fix it to a convenient place on the box.

Your finished toolbox should look like this when complete

DVD RACK

Here is a simple design for a rack to keep all your discs safely. It will accommodate both CD cases and DVD boxes. It is not difficult to make but relies on accurate halving joints for stability. If you need more space it is easy to expand, and you could even fit a timber or glass shelf to the top to support your television.

DVD RACK

- Table saw or handsaw

- Chisel

- Biscuit jointer

- Biscuits

- Clamps

- Wood glue

5¹⁄₂ in (140mm)

5¹⁄₂in (140mm)

13³⁄₁₆ in (335mm)

⁴⁄₅in (20mm)

2³⁄₄in (70mm)

2³⁄₄in (70mm)

13³⁄₁₆ in (335mm)

⁴⁄₅ in (20mm)

7¹⁄₄ in (185mm)

55in (1395mm)

13³⁄₁₆ in (335mm)

27¹⁄₈ in (690mm)

2³⁄₄in (70mm)

5¹⁄₈ in (130mm)

⁴⁄₅in (20mm)

7¹⁄₄ in (185mm)

⁴⁄₅in (20mm)

5⁷⁄₈in (150mm)

5⁷⁄₈in (150mm)

5⁷⁄₈in (150mm)

5⁷⁄₈in (150mm)

8¹⁄₃in (220mm)

⁴⁄₅ in (20mm)

5⁷⁄₈in (150mm)

5⁷⁄₈in (150mm)

⁴⁄₅ in (20mm)

2³⁄₄in (70mm)

8¹⁄₃ in (220mm)

Begin by marking out your board as shown here.

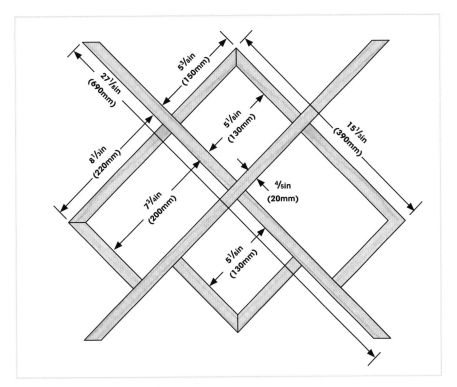

Front view with measurements

- 5³⁄₈in (150mm)
- 27¹⁄₈in (690mm)
- 5¹⁄₈in (130mm)
- 15¹⁄₃in (390mm)
- 8¹⁄₃in (220mm)
- 7³⁄₄in (200mm)
- ⁴⁄₅in (20mm)
- 5¹⁄₈in (130mm)

1 Prepare your plank as described on page 19. The boards all have mitred ends, and the easiest way to cut these is using a table saw (as here). However, you could also use a portable circular saw or a handsaw.

2 Once you have cut the boards to length, mark out the halving joints. Take an offcut of the plank to ensure that they are exactly the right width.

3 The marked joints should look like this.

4 Again the table saw is a good way to cut these joints; however, a handsaw is equally effective.

5 Work your way across the joint. Remember that the circular blade cuts at an angle, so leave a space in front of the marked line.

6 Pare out the waste with a chisel.

7 The simplest way to hold the mitred joints together is to use biscuits. Set your jointer fence to 45 degrees and cut a single slot in the mitred end of each board.

8 For the lowest section of the CD rack you also need to cut joints in the board ends where they join onto the main frame. To do this place the short board in position on the longer board. Mark a line across the long board at the rear of the short board. Now fold the short board back on the line and clamp it in position on the long board. Mark the centre of the board and line up the jointer horizontally on it using the base plate as the reference face. Cut a slot.

9 Then stand the jointer vertically on the board with its base against the slot that you have just cut and cut another slot in the long board.

10 The finished joint awaiting a biscuit.

11 To assemble the rack, start by making the biscuit joint and gluing the two short boards together. Clamp them in position if necessary.

12 Next apply glue to the halving joint on the two long boards and the halving joints on the shorter boards. Carefully slide the assembly together. A few gentle taps with a mallet may be needed.

13 Fit the two short end boards in position with biscuits and then take the final two boards and glue them together. Before the glue has cured fit them onto the main frame with the two biscuit joints. Clamp in position if necessary.

Your finished DVD rack should look like this when complete

SHOE RACK

Here is a design for a simple shoe rack. It will keep your shoes neatly out of the way and takes up little space. It is easy to make but relies on tight joints to keep it secure, so take care when cutting them.

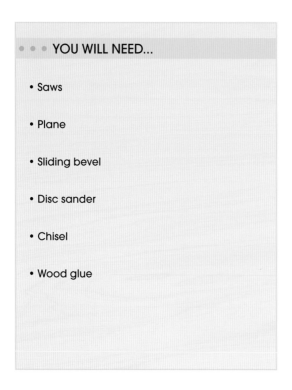

SHOE RACK

● ● ● YOU WILL NEED...

- Saws

- Plane

- Sliding bevel

- Disc sander

- Chisel

- Wood glue

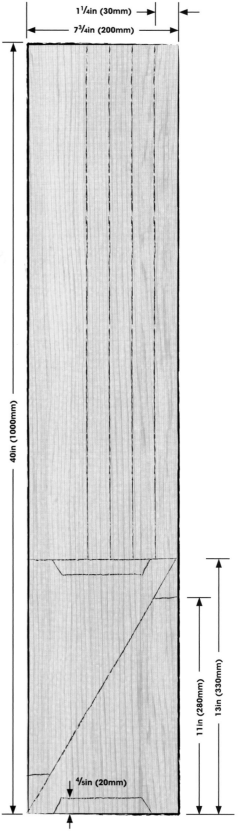

1¼in (30mm)

7¾in (200mm)

40in (1000mm)

11in (280mm)

13in (330mm)

⁴⁄₅in (20mm)

Begin by marking out your board as shown here

1 Prepare your plank as described on page 19. Mark up the plank and then crosscut the end piece that makes up the two sides.

2 Cut the piece diagonally. This is an easy job for a bandsaw, but you could use a handsaw or jigsaw if you prefer.

3 Tape the two pieces together, then place in a vice and plane both the sawn edges at the same time to make the pieces identical.

4 Now mark the cutout for the feet. Use a sliding bevel to mirror the slope of the front and make each foot 1¼in (30mm) wide. Join the two with a horizontal line 4/5in (20mm) up from the base.

5 The tip of the triangular sides needs to be removed, so mark a horizontal line 10¼in (260mm) from the base and saw the top off.

6 Again, the bandsaw can be used for shaping the feet, although a jigsaw or coping saw would also do the job.

7 Rip the four rails. They are all 1¼in (30mm) wide.

8 Now mark the joints. These are set ⅖in (10mm) in from the ends of the rails. The simplest method is to lay the rails flat on the bench and then stand the ends upon them. Mark the joints with a pencil.

9 Use a tenon saw to cut down the sides of the joint. They should all be about 15/32in (12mm) deep. Make a cut on each side of the joint and then several across the width.

10 Pare out the waste with a chisel.

11 Form a small chamfer around the exposed ends of the rails. A disc sander is the ideal tool for this, but you could use a block plane or even a chisel to achieve the same result.

12 The joints alone should hold the rails in position tightly, so only a dab of glue is needed.

13 The precise position of the rails is not critical.

Your finished shoe rack should look like this when complete

CLOTHES AIRER

Drying clothes can be a chore. You can't rely on the weather, and the dryer costs a lot to run, so why not use a simple clothes airer that can be placed next to a radiator or perhaps the kitchen range to provide economical and efficient drying. Here is a straightforward design that uses traditional jointing to make a useful and convenient unit that can be expanded to meet your needs. This design uses three identical frames.

CLOTHES AIRER

• • • YOU WILL NEED...

- Saws

- Plane

- Clamps

- Mortise-marking gauge

- Chisels

- Disc sander

- Wood glue

7in (180mm)

35$\frac{1}{2}$in (900mm)

22in (560mm)

71in (1805mm)

22in (560mm)

$^{4}/_{5}$in (20mm)

35$\frac{1}{2}$in (900mm)

$^{4}/_{5}$in (20mm)

22in (560mm)

Begin by marking out your board as shown here

1 Prepare your plank as described on page 19. Once you crosscut and ripped the components, you will need to clean up the edges, so use a plane (as here) or a sander.

2 Take the six uprights and clamp them all together. Use a try square to line them up and a 'G' or 'F' clamp to hold them in position.

3 The top rail should be located ⁴⁄₅in (20mm) from the top of the upright. Use a try square to mark the position.

4 Use the rail to mark the exact width. Repeat for the lower rail, this time 19¾in (500mm) below the top.

5 The frames are held together using mortise and tenon joints. To mark the joints you need to use a mortise-marking gauge. Set the width of the pins to match your chisel.

6 Mark the position of the joints on the uprights at ⁴⁄₅in (20mm) and 19¾in (500mm) from the top.

7 Use a pencil to mark the length of the joints, using one of the rails as a guide.

8 Mark the tenon width on the ends of the rails, again using the mortise gauge with the same settings as before.

9 Mark the tenon shoulders with a try square. The tenons can go all the way through the stiles, but it is neater to make them stop short.

10 Use a chisel and mallet to pare away the waste in the uprights, working your way down to the base of the mortise in stages.

11 Stand the rails vertically in a vice and use a tenon saw or pullsaw to saw down the tenon cheeks. Be careful to keep to the waste side of the marked line.

12 Cut the shoulders.

13 Test-fit the joints. You may need to shave a little off the tenon with a chisel to make it a snug fit.

14 The joint must fit tightly up to the shoulders.

15 The tops of the uprights should be rounded over. Anything round and an appropriate size can be used to mark them. Then shape the curves with a disc sander.

16 Dry assemble each of the frames and make sure that all the joints fit and that the frames are square. When you are satisfied, apply a little glue to the joints and then clamp up and leave to set.

17 To hinge the frames you can either fit metal hinges, make some fabric hinges or, alternatively, use a pair of thick rubber bands like these.

Your finished clothes airer should look like this when complete

WINE RACK

You never know when you might feel the need to celebrate, so it makes sense to keep a few good bottles of wine ready for that moment. You don't need to be a connoisseur to know that to keep wine at its best it should be stored horizontally so that the cork is kept moist. Here is a simple rack to hold eight bottles. There is some curved cutting to do so you will need a narrow blade for your jigsaw or bandsaw. Alternatively you could use a coping saw.

WINE RACK

● ● ● YOU WILL NEED...

- Pair of compasses

- Saws

- Drum sander

- Biscuit jointer (with both No. 20 and No. 10 biscuits)

- Router table and rounding-over cutter

- Clamps

- Wood glue

Begin by marking out your board as shown here

7in (180mm)

13³/₄in (350mm)

2¹/₃in (60mm)

18¹/₈in (460mm)

2³/₄in (70mm)

R: ⁴/₅in (20mm)

R: 1¹/₂ in (40mm)

18¹/₈in (460mm)

69¹/₃ in (177mm)

2³/₄ in (70mm)

4¹/₃in (110mm)

3¹/₈in (80mm)

13³/₄in (350mm)

2¹/₃in (60mm)

1 Prepare your plank as described on page 19. When marking out your board, make allowances if you are likely to be storing sparkling wine in sturdier bottles or bottles that are larger (or smaller) than standard sizes.

3 Now you need to use a compass to mark the curved supports for the bottles. For the two rear bars set the radius to 1½in (40mm), and for the two front bars set the radius to ⅘in (20mm).

2 Once you've cut out your components, take the four bars that support the bottles and lay them on the bench. On the two rear bars mark a horizontal line ⅘in (20mm) up from the bottom. On the front two mark a horizontal line 1¾in (45mm) up from the bottom. Line up all the boards together perfectly square. Mark the centre lines for the bottle cutouts. Work in from one end and mark one line 2⅓in (60mm) in, and a second a further 4⅞in (113mm) in. Repeat the procedure from the other end. Mark these lines across all four bars simultaneously.

4 With the compass point on one of the vertical lines draw a semicircle so that its circumference just touches the horizontal line where the two lines cross. Repeat for all four cutouts and do the same for the front bars using the smaller radius.

5 Clamp the bars to the workbench and carefully cut out the curves with a coping saw, bandsaw or jigsaw (as here) fitted with a narrow blade.

6 These will look a bit rough, so clean them up with a small drum sander mounted in a pillar drill or a power drill.

7 The next job is to make the side frames. These are very simple and made in the form of an H. The horizontal bar is just biscuit jointed into the two uprights. Arrange the components accurately and mark the positions of the two biscuits. Clamp the components to the workbench and cut the joint. For this joint you should use No. 20 biscuits. Apply glue to the slots and assemble the two ends. Clamp up securely until dry.

8 All the parts of the wine rack, including the support bars, should have their edges smoothed and rounded. The simplest way to achieve this is to use a bearing-guided rounding-over cutter in a router table. Work along the curved edges and then turn the workpiece over and repeat on the other side. Round over the bottom edges and ends as well.

9 The cutter cannot get tight into corners, so there is always a small section that is left square. You can easily round this off with a little abrasive paper.

10 You are now ready to assemble the rack. For this joint, No. 10 biscuits should be used. Start by marking the central line on all the bottle support rails. Then mark a line 2in (50mm) in from the ends of the side frames. Stand the support rails on the side frames with their bottom edges on the marked lines. Now mark off the position of the biscuit on the frame.

11 Use a try square to transfer the marks across to the second end frame.

12 Set your jointer for No.10 biscuits and cut the slots in the ends of all the rails.

13 Because the rails need to be set back on the end frames, you need to reset the jointer fence so that it is ⅕in (5mm) further away from the blade. Then clamp the end frame in a vice with the inside face towards you and cut the slot for the biscuits using the lines you marked earlier. It is easier to see them if you extend them onto the edges of the uprights with a try square.

14 Once all the joints are cut you are ready to start the assembly. However, before you do so, spend a little time cleaning up all the components with some abrasive paper or a power sander to remove the pencil marks and any other blemishes.

15 Assembly is straightforward. Apply a little glue to each of the biscuit slots, insert the biscuits and fit the rails. Make sure that all the rails are correctly set 2in (50mm) from the ends of the side frames. Use four bar clamps to hold the rack together while the glue cures.

Your finished wine rack should look like this when complete

STEP-UP

There are times when we all need a little help to reach that top shelf or change the light bulb or, if you are very young, just to reach the sink! Here is a design for a little pair of steps that would be ideal in the kitchen or perhaps in the bathroom for the younger family members. The jointing is all done using a pocket-hole jig, which makes it simple to assemble. However, you could use biscuit joints if you prefer.

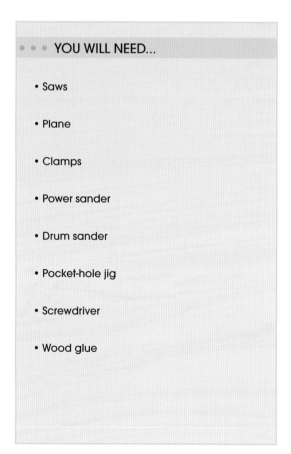

STEP-UP

• • • YOU WILL NEED...

- Saws

- Plane

- Clamps

- Power sander

- Drum sander

- Pocket-hole jig

- Screwdriver

- Wood glue

12in (300mm)

12½in (320mm)

11in (280mm)

5½in (140mm)

11in (280mm)

11in (280mm)

2⅓in (60mm)

5⅞in (150mm)

46⅞in (1190mm)

11in (280mm)

5⅛in (130mm)

2in (50mm)

R: 4in (100mm)

7in (180mm)

R: 4in (100mm)

2in (50mm)

5⅞in (150mm)

Begin by marking out your board as shown here

1 Prepare your plank as described on page 19. Mark out your plank. Depending on your plank, you may need to join several pieces to make up the sides, so divide the board into sensible widths to make an oversize panel that can be trimmed to size later. Alternatively cut the sides out as a single piece.

2 First crosscut the components to length, then rip them to width. Both these steps can be achieved with a handsaw, if you do not have a table saw (as here).

3 Before jointing the boards to make up the sides, plane the edges so that they fit together neatly.

4 Apply a little glue to each of the joints. It is only necessary to apply glue to one edge of the joint.

5 Clamp the board up and allow the glue to cure, then clean up any roughness with a power sander.

6 Trim the panel to size then mark two lines on the board, one vertical 5⅞in (150mm) in from the front edge and another horizontal 5⅞in (150mm) down from the top edge.

7 You could simply make a square cutout, but a curve looks better. A 7¾in (200mm) diameter saucepan lid was used here as a template to make the curve.

8 The lid was used again to mark the curve between the feet. Draw two vertical lines 2in (50mm) in from the front and back edges and position the lid between them to draw the curve.

9 Once both end panels are marked out ready for cutting, clamp the panel so that it is overhanging the edge of the workbench and use a powered jigsaw (as here) or coping saw to cut out the curves. If you have a long enough blade, you could clamp both sides together and cut at the same time.

10 Use a small drum sander in a pillar drill or on a power drill to smooth the curves and remove any saw marks. Then soften all the sharp edges with some abrasive paper.

11 All the joints are pocket holes and are machined using the simple jig shown. Make a pair of holes in the ends of each rail and three holes along the top of each rail.

12 Lay one side panel on the bench and screw the rails into position.

13 Set the rails back a little way from the edge of the side panel, as this produces a much neater appearance.

14 The completed frame.

15 Invert the frame and screw the steps into position.

16 Carefully go over the whole piece with abrasive paper, removing any blemishes or sharp edges so that it all feels smooth to the touch.

Your finished step-up should look like this when complete

CORNER SHELVES

The corner of a room is often wasted space, but it is, in fact, an excellent place to hang shelves either for display or storage. Corner shelving can look a little dull using the usual triangular shelves and rounded front edges, so here is a slightly more unusual design that also provides versatile and decorative storage.

CORNER SHELVES

12in (300mm)

4¹⁄₃in (110mm)

7¹⁄₂in (190mm)

7¹⁄₂in (190mm)

7¹⁄₂in (190mm)

7¹⁄₂in (190mm)

7¹⁄₂in (190mm)

31¹⁄₂in (800mm)

7¹⁄₂in (190mm)

67³⁄₄in (1720mm)

2in (50mm)

Begin by marking out your board as shown here

1 Prepare your plank as described on page 19. Cut out your components, then line up the four uprights and clamp them together. Mark off the positions of the shelves across all four at the same time. The spacing chosen here is approximately 7½in (190mm) with 4in (100mm) left at each end.

2 You must rout out the housings in the uprights to hold the shelves. Choose a cutter that matches the thickness of your shelves; alternatively you could choose a smaller cutter and move your guide fence to cut a wider groove. A third option is to plane your shelves to match the width of whatever cutter you have.

3 Keep the uprights clamped together and position them over the edge of the bench. Clamp a board across them to act as a guide for the router. You will need to stand your router on the boards with the cutter just touching the surface on the marked line in order to set the correct distance for the board to be set. Once you have set the distance for the guide board, you need to adjust the depth of cut. It should be roughly two-thirds of the depth of the upright.

4 Make sure that the uprights are securely held in position and then machine the groove across them. Do not cut to full depth in one go, but take several shallow passes until you reach full depth.

5 After machining the groove you may need to clean up the edges with abrasive paper to remove any rough edges.

6 The completed uprights.

7 For a neat appearance, it is worth rounding over the edges of the uprights. The simplest method of doing this is to use a bearing-guided rounding-over cutter mounted in a router table. Use the mitre fence to mould the ends of the rails first, then mould the sides.

8 Next make the shelves. For the large shelf on the bottom you may need to joint a couple of pieces. Before jointing, plane the edges smooth to make a snug joint. Apply glue to one edge then clamp up tight and leave to dry.

9 The protruding corners of the shelves should be rounded off. Use a suitable round object as a template.

10 Use a jigsaw or coping saw (as here) to cut the curve, then smooth it off with a disc sander.

11 The shelving unit is held together using screws. Drill a ⁵⁄₃₂in (4mm) hole through the centre of each housing in the uprights.

12 Countersink the holes on the reverse side.

13 Start assembling the shelves from the top down. Set the outer uprights flush with the edge of the top shelf and the inner uprights close to the inner corner, leaving a gap between them.

Your finished corner shelves should look like this when complete

GLOSSARY

Bandsaw Stationary workshop machine that uses a continuous blade running round two or sometimes three bandwheels and through a metal worktable. Can be used for cutting complex curved shapes and also joints.

Bar clamp Long clamp used on wide assemblies and panels.

Bearing-guided cutter Router cutter with integral roller bearing that runs against workpiece to produce a consistent depth of cut.

Bench hook Workshop-made jig to hold timber securely when crosscutting, especially when using a tenon saw.

Bevel A slope, such as the sharpening angle on a blade or a sloping edge on a piece of timber, often used for decoration.

Biscuit Oval-shaped, flat, compressed-timber dowel used in conjunction with a biscuit jointer. When used with water-based glue such as PVA, the biscuit will swell making a very secure joint. Available in several sizes to suit different timber thicknesses.

Block plane Small plane with a low-angled blade used on end grain and for chamfering edges.

Chamfer Similar to a bevel but cut symmetrically to both surfaces at 45 degrees.

Clearance hole Hole bored through a timber component that is being fixed. The hole must be large enough to accommodate the widest part of the screw thread without it engaging.

Combination square Metal tool combining the functions of a try square, mitre square and steel rule.

Coping saw Small frame saw with a narrow blade for cutting curves.

Crosscutting Sawing across the grain of the timber, reducing the length of a board.

Crown guard Metal or plastic guard fitted to a table saw to cover the top of the blade that would otherwise be left exposed during cutting.

Countersink bit Conical drill bit that creates a funnel-shaped recess at the top of a drilled hole to allow the screw head to sit flush with or below the surface.

Dowel Circular peg or cylindrical length of timber.

Dust extractor Modified vacuum cleaner with high-powered motor and fine-filtration system. Often incorporates autoswitching, so it works in sync with the on–off switch of the connected tool.

End grain The fibres at the end of a board that are exposed by crosscutting.

'F' clamp Also known as a speed clamp. A sliding clamp head runs on a serrated bar making it fast to use and quick to adjust.

Fence Guide used on a power tool or machine to align the workpiece accurately in relation to the cutter.

'G' clamp So called because it looks like the letter 'G'. A simple, straightforward, reliable clamp for general use.

Guide rail Alloy rail designed to be used with power tools such as routers and circular saws to steer them accurately across a workpiece.

Halving joint Joint that is used when joining two components of identical thickness. Half the thickness is taken from each component and the pair will then fit together with their faces flush.

Hardpoint saw Panel saw with hardened, razor-sharp teeth that can be used for both ripping and crosscutting. Fast cutting, but cannot be sharpened once blunted.

Hardwood Timber produced by deciduous trees such as oak or ash. Not always hard – balsa is classed as a hardwood.

Hone To produce a finely sharpened edge using an abrasive stone.

Housing joint Joint where one component is housed in a slot in another, for example, in a bookshelf. The upright would have a housing cut in it into which the shelf would fit.

Kerf The gap in the timber left by a saw blade.

Mallet Hammer-type tool with a wooden, or sometimes rubber, striking head. Used for driving chisels into hardwood and also for knocking joints together.

Marking gauge A wooden gauge for marking lines parallel to a work-piece edge.

MDF Medium Density Fibreboard – a manufactured board made from compressed timber particles. Has a very smooth surface, ideal for painting.

Mitre box Wooden or plastic jig with accurate slots cut into it to guide a handsaw for precise angled crosscutting.

Mitre fence Sliding fence on a table saw used for angled crosscutting.

Mortise and tenon Traditional timber joint with a peg (tenon) formed on one component and a socket (mortise) cut into the other.

Pilot hole Hole bored in timber to accommodate the screw shank but not the thread. Used to ease screw insertion and prevent timber from splitting.

Plywood Manufactured board made from gluing several thin layers or 'plies' together to make a strong, stable material.

Pocket hole Angled screw hole used to join two pieces of timber together with a self-boring screw. Usually drilled using a special jig.

Push stick Length of timber or plastic with a notched end used to move a workpiece past a blade or cutters without risk to an operator's hands.

Pullsaw A thin-bladed saw that, unlike conventional saws, cuts only on the pull stroke. Of Japanese origin but now widely available everywhere.

PVA Polyvinyl acetate – a water-based wood glue ideal for general use.

Rail The horizontal component in a frame. A stool would have rails between its legs.

Rebate A step-shaped recess cut on the edge of a workpiece. Often made to fit a corresponding slot on a neighbouring piece.

Ripping Sawing parallel to the grain of the timber along the length of a board.

Riving knife Crescent-shaped plate mounted behind the blade of a circular saw to hold the kerf open and stop the timber binding on the blade. Often also used to support the crown guard.

Softwood Timber produced by coniferous trees such as pine.

Side grain This refers to the grain that runs parallel to the side of the board. Gluing side grain to side grain produces a strong joint.

Sliding bevel Adjustable tool used for marking angles and setting machinery blades and fences.

Smoothing plane Mid-sized plane ideal for general use.

Table saw Stationary workshop machine with a circular saw blade mounted in a metal table. Guide fences are used to guide the workpiece accurately past the blade.

Tenon saw Small fine-toothed saw used for joint cutting and bench work. Usually has a metal stiffening strip along the back of the blade for extra rigidity. For this reason it is also called a back saw.

Try square L-shaped tool designed for marking 90-degree angles using the workpiece edge as a reference.

Web clamp Used for clamping irregular shapes. It has a ratcheted strap and can incorporate corner pieces as required.

CONVERSION CHART

Imperial to metric						Metric to imperial	
Inches (fractions)	Inches (decimal)	Millimetres (decimal)	Inches (fractions)	Inches (decimal)	Millimetres (decimal)	Millimetres (decimal)	Inches (decimal)
1/64	0.0156	0.3969	33/64	0.5156	13.0969	1	0.0394
1/32	0.0313	0.7938	17/32	0.5313	13.4938	1.5	0.0591
3/64	0.0469	1.1906	35/64	0.5469	13.8906	2	0.0787
1/16	0.0625	1.5875	9/16	0.5625	14.2875	2.5	0.0984
5/64	0.0781	1.9844	37/64	0.5781	14.6844	3	0.1181
3/32	0.0938	2.3813	19/32	0.5938	15.0813	3.5	0.1378
7/64	0.1094	2.7781	39/64	0.6094	15.4781	4	0.1575
1/8	0.1250	3.1750	5/8	0.6250	15.8750	4.5	0.1772
9/64	0.1406	3.5719	41/64	0.6406	16.2719	5	0.1969
5/32	0.1563	3.9688	21/32	0.6563	16.6688	5.5	0.2165
11/64	0.1719	4.3656	43/64	0.6719	17.0656	6	0.2362
3/16	0.1875	4.7625	11/16	0.6875	17.4625	6.5	0.2559
13/64	0.2031	5.1594	45/64	0.7031	17.8594	7	0.2756
7/32	0.2188	5.5563	23/32	0.7188	18.2563	7.5	0.2953
15/64	0.2344	5.9531	47/64	0.7344	18.6531	8	0.3150
1/4	0.2500	6.3500	3/4	0.7500	19.0500	8.5	0.3346
17/64	0.2656	6.7469	49/64	0.7656	19.4469	9	0.3543
7/32	0.2813	7.1438	25/32	0.7813	19.8438	9.5	0.3740
19/64	0.2969	7.5406	51/64	0.7969	20.2406	10	0.3937
5/16	0.3125	7.9375	13/16	0.8125	20.6375	10.5	0.4134
21/64	0.3281	8.3344	53/64	0.8281	21.0344	11	0.4331
11/32	0.3438	8.7313	27/32	0.8438	21.4313	11.5	0.4528
23/64	0.3594	9.1281	55/64	0.8594	21.8281	12	0.4724
3/8	0.3750	9.5250	7/8	0.8750	22.2250	12.5	0.4921
25/64	0.3906	9.9219	57/64	0.8906	22.6219	13	0.5118
13/32	0.4063	10.3188	29/32	0.9063	23.0188	13.5	0.5315
27/64	0.4219	10.7156	59/64	0.9219	23.4156	14	0.5512
7/16	0.4375	11.1125	15/16	0.9375	23.8125	14.5	0.5709
29/64	0.4531	11.5094	61/64	0.9531	24.2094	15	0.5906
15/32	0.4688	11.9063	31/32	0.9688	24.6063	15.5	0.6102
31/64	0.4844	12.3031	63/64	0.9844	25.0031	16	0.6299
1/2	0.5000	12.7000	1	1.0000	25.4000	16.5	0.6496

ABOUT THE AUTHOR

Trained furniture maker Andy Standing has been writing magazine articles on woodworking techniques and projects for the past 15 years. He is a regular contributor to "The Woodworker", "Furniture & Cabinetmaking", "Woodworking Plans & Projects" and "Practical Woodworking".

His career in woodturning began in the 1990s when he left his role as a studio manager for BBC Radio in London and moved to Norfolk with his young family. Andy took a City and Guilds course in furniture making and achieved the level of distinction. He subsequently set up his own workshop and began making furniture to commission. He continued this for some years while at the same time writing occasional articles for woodworking magazines. Gradually he has found himself spending more time in front of his laptop and less in front of his workbench.

In this book for home woodworkers, Andy aims to provide the reader with a useful range of projects that can be simply made using easily obtainable materials. The projects vary in complexity but most can easily be completed by any novice to intermediate woodworker.

By the end of the book, Andy hopes the reader will have managed to make some useful items for themselves and also learnt a few new woodworking techniques along the way.

INDEX

To order a book or request a catalogue, contact:
GMC Publications Ltd.
Castle Place, 166 High Street, Lewes, East Sussex, BN7 1XU, United Kingdom
Tel: +44 (0)1273 488005   Fax: +44 (0)1273 402866   www.gmcbooks.com